The Tradition of Masks in Indian Culture

The Tradition of Masks in Indian Culture

An Anthropological Study of Majuli, Assam

Arifur Zaman

Indira Gandhi Rashtriya Manav Sangrahalaya
Bhopal

Aryan Books International
New Delhi

The Tradition of Masks in Indian Culture

ISBN: 978-81-7305-520-1

Published in **2015** by

Indira Gandhi Rashtriya Manav Sangrahalaya

Shamla Hills, Bhopal - 462 013 (M.P.)

and

Aryan Books International

Pooja Apartments, 4B, Ansari Road, New Delhi-110 002 (India)

Tel.: 23287589, 23255799; Fax: 91-11-23270385

E-mail: aryanbooks@gmail.com

www.aryanbooks.co.in

Designed and Printed in India by

ABI Prints & Publishing Co., New Delhi

Unveiling the Mask

A mask is a painted or engraved piece of object generally worn over the face to hide one's identity and to reveal as another man, animal, mythological creature, etc. Hiding one's identity and revealing as another being is the inevitable feature of mask. Mask transforms something from natural to cultural trait. A mask is invariably worn with an integral costume. Sometimes a face is cemented with cosmetics or colours as the person tries to hide or improve his appearance. Colouring of performers' faces instead of covering with masks is generally done to fulfill the necessities of dance and dramas. Such a painting is known as pliant mask. Some shrewd persons try to hide their mischievous and anti-social activities camouflaging as benevolent persons. They are known as 'masked men' in our society.

From the remote past masks are related to the primordial thought process indispensably related to the innumerable cultures. Moreover, masks are integral to each civilization. Mask making tradition have been dispersed throughout the world ever since the early diffusion of *Homo sapiens*. Although a mask is generally worn over the face as a form of disguise, some of those almost cover the entire body of the wearer. Some of the huge masks are divided into a number of separable parts. Beliefs and superstitious about masks abound in many societies. These artificial faces also play pivotal role in the socio-cultural study of a community which has a tradition of making and using of masks.

The known masks from the rock art, prehistoric and protohistoric remains to the present time could be divided into two broad categories:

(i) Anthropomorphic mask: those are derived from human features, and

(ii) Theriomorphic mask: which are derived from animal features

However, there are some masks like Narasimha, one of the incarnations of Lord Vishnu, which is the combination of man (anthropomorphic) and lion (theriomorphic). The earliest evidences of mask are found in the rock shelters and cave walls of the Upper Paleolithic Period created by our hunter ancestors to fulfill their magico-religious needs. The limitation of the early men to control the nature and to overcome the uncertainty and acute obstacles of life are probably the causes behind the creation of mask. Such hindrances and uncertainty are still present in the today's so called advanced society. Therefore, probably like the primitive men, the people of advanced societies also take resort to mask, through which, they believed obstacles of life could be overcome. Therefore, mask tradition continued even after hunter primitive men entered into the higher form of culture.

From time immemorial, Assam has a thought provoking heritage of making and using masks. Due to dearth of the prehistoric evidence, it is difficult to speak on the antiquity of the glorious tradition of mask in Assam. The mask makers of Assam use the materials easily available in the environment like bamboo, wood, etc. to fulfill their aesthetic need; among those the masks made of bamboo spilt easily caught the pleasing eye of the viewers due to their intricate and splendid features. Moreover, such masks are very light in comparison to their size, for which the wearers can carry those without much difficulty. The size of the clay pot or a wooden log restricts the imagination of the mask maker, because he has to complete the mask within the limitation of the material; but the maker who uses bamboo split to create a mask could materialize his imagination as it is easy to add bamboo split one after another to make a huge mask. To make this type of mask bamboo split made basket woven in open six point star pattern is covered by cotton cloth and coated with a mixture of clay, cowdung and water and after drying finally coloured and embellished.

The masks, especially the bamboo split made masks, are integral to the Vaishnavism of Assam. The great saint Srimanta Sankaradeva (1449-1568) propagated Neo-Vaishnavism in North East India, which was a part of the larger pan-Indian resurgence of unflinching devotion *(bhakti)*. Dance and dramas are indispensable parts of the Vaishnavism of this remote part of India. Besides various prayers, the supreme deity of Vaishnavism, Lord Vishnu, the preserver and the restorer, is also propitiated through dance and dramas by the Vaishnavas of Assam. According to their belief the heaven *(swarga, vaikuntha)* is seven tiered. Once the devotee *(bhaktas)* requested Sankaradeva to explain the *sapta* (seven) *vaikuntha* (heaven). Then Sankaradeva thought that it would be better to show something instead of explaining again and again about the features of heaven. Then he wrote a drama *(nat)* entitled *Cihna Yatra,* where he exhibited some paintings of heaven drawn by himself and used masks to depict some of the characters. The *Cihna Yatra* is the first Vaishnavite drama of Assam, and there the great Guru initiated the use of masks to depict some of the non-human characters. From that time mask became part and parcel of the Vaishnavite ritualistic dance and drama. Probably bamboo split woven mask initiated its journey from the performance of *Cinha Yatra.*

It is unfortunate that till today elaborate systematic micro-study has not been conducted on this praiseworthy tradition of Assam. Dr. Arifur Zaman is the first one, who painstakingly undertook the study of mask at Natun Chamaguri Satra of Majuli, the riverine island of Assam. It is pertinent to note that Majuli is the nerve-centre of Assam's Vaishnavism, where the eye-catching tradition of mask making is nourished in the four *satras* (Vaishnavite monasteries). Dr. Zaman had meticulously churned the heritage of the Natun Chamaguri Satra, and the precious outcome is the book entitled *The Tradition of Masks in Indian Culture: An Anthropological Study of Majuli, Assam.*

The study is well executed. The methodological steps are appropriate and the empirical data collected by the author are well presented and discussed. The literature review integral to the study is robust. Dr. Zaman's knowledge and use of existing literature are not in doubt, which is clearly demonstrated in the discussion and findings. The study has conspicuously contributed to the knowledge by exploring the heritage of mask at Majuli, the process as well as the different type of masks in the study area. The endeavour also has shown the economic, social, cultural and religious significance of the masks and a praiseworthy record of the available masks of the Natun Chamaguri Satra.

Dr. Zaman is an enthusiastic and energetic young man with an academic bent of mind, presently working as Assistant Professor of Anthropology in Dibrugarh University, Assam. I sincerely believe that this empirical micro-study will pave the way for further studies on the ignored traits of the sacred complexes of this lesser known part of India.

Birinchi K. Medhi

Contents

Preface

Mask is an integral object of culture complex in many societies in a cross-cultural perspective. It is one of the forms of camouflages which conceal one's factual and natural identity and reveal the identity of another being. Masks have a great influence on human society and among some, it is conspicuously related with religious, socio-economic, as well as cultural aspects. The study under consideration was carried out in one of the important Vaishnavite *satras* (monastery or *math*) of Majuli, situated at Jorhat district of Assam. The concerned *satra* has a praiseworthy tradition of mask making whose aesthetic insinuation as well as confessions of the maker have attracted visitors from many parts of the world. They also stand as one of the proud components of cultural heritage of Assam as well as for the whole of the country. They are considered as august and egotistical archetype of their master's creation. The mask makers are endowed with dignified appellation like Sangeet Nataka Academy Award conferred by the Government of India, awarded artist pension by the state government, etc. for their praiseworthy skills. The Natun Chamaguri Satra is also known as Majuli Chamaguri Satra. The villagers, where the *satra* is located, are engaged in many economic activities like agriculture, government services, teaching, petty trade, etc. in order to maintain their day-to-day life. Basic data for the present study was mainly collected from the study *of* this *satra* and cross-verification was made with other mask making *satras* of Majuli; these include Alengi Narasimha Satra, Bihimpur Satra and Prachin Chamaguri Satra.

At the very outset I would like to express my indebtedness to my guide as well as philosopher, who is independently and also collectively instrumental for what I am today. My heartiest thanks and gratitude goes to Dr. Birinchi K. Medhi, Professor of Anthropology, Gauhati University, for guiding and helping me to undertake the study. His erudition and scholarship has been a great source of inspiration to me. I would remain beholden to him because without his learned guidance, the study would not have seen the light of the day. This study, perhaps, could not have been completed without the constant inspiration that I received from Dr. Zoii Nath Sarmah, Executive President and Director, North Eastern Regional Institute of Management, Guwahati. He not only encouraged me and strengthened my resolve to carry on with the study, but also showered me with all possible help and facilities. I am extremely grateful to him. My heartfelt thanks also goes to Mr. Abani Borthakur, Census Compiler, Directorate of Census Operation, Assam, for providing me with every possible help regarding the latest census data.

I would like to take this opportunity to thank the lovable people of the Natun Chamaguri Village, Majuli, young and old, for their full cooperation and help, without whom my field-work would not have been possible. I am grateful to Sri Sri Koshakanta Deva Goswami, the *Satradhikar* of the Natun Chamaguri Satra, and his family members, for their untiring help and inspiration. I am also thankful to Sri Hem Chandra Goswami, a mask maker of repute, Sri Krishna Goswami, Artist and Lecturer, Government Art College, Guwahati, without whose help it would not have been possible for me to complete this venture. I am also indebted to Sri Sri Janardan Deva Goswami, *Satradhikar*, Uttar Kamalabari Satra, Majuli, and Mr. Hiteshwar Bora, a social activist of Majuli, who were of great help and inspiration to me during my stay at Majuli through their hospitality as well as scholaristic attitudes. A large number of individuals as well as *bhaktas* (devotees) and other personnels of different *satras* of Majuli, employees of different offices and establishments helped and assisted me in completing the study. Despite their normal preoccupations and official duties, they always found the time to cooperate with me wholeheartedly during the course of this study. I owe my deep sense of gratitude to them. I offer my sincere apology for not being able to name each one of them here.

I offer my heartfelt thanks to Ms. Asha Gupta of Indira Gandhi National Centre for the Arts, New Delhi, for guiding me during my library work there. I am thankful to the staff of the libraries of Gauhati University, National Institute of Rural Development, Omeo Kumar Das Institute of Social Change and Development, District Library, Guwahati, Library of North Eastern Regional Institute of Management, Cotton College Library, Arya Vidyapeeth College Library, National Institute of People's Co-operation and Child Development, Assam, Institute of Research for Tribals and Scheduled Castes, and others for enabling me to do a literature survey and to collect the required data. I am indebted to the museum personnel of Srimanta Sankaradeva Kalakshetra, Assam State Museum, Madhab Chandra Goswami Museum of Anthropology Department, Gauhati University, National Museum of Delhi, Salar Jang Museum of Hyderabad, Indira Gandhi Rashtriya Manav Sangrahalaya, Bhopal, etc. which I visited for gathering data regarding masks as well as art forms of different cultures of the world.

I feel immense pleasure in expressing my gratitude to Indira Gandhi Rashtriya Manav Sangrahalaya, Bhopal. This esteemed organisation is the main catalyst to transform my study into an eye-catching book. I must put an record my deep sense of gratitude towards Prof. K.K. Misra, the then director of IGRMS, and all the concerned persons of the organisation.

I owe a lot to my family members and my sincere thanks are reserved for my father, Sri Mohammad Ali, whose help and immense patience in all directions saw me through. I extend my sincere thanks to all those individuals and establishments whose names cannot be included here for dearth of space but who have helped me in one way or the other during the course of the study.

Arifur Zaman

List of Figures

List of Plates

1

Introduction

1.1 PRELUDE

Masks are artificial faces worn for disguise, generally to assume and to frighten. They are often worn to conceal feelings and also as coverings to hide or protect the faces. They may be carved, moulded, or even woven objects, which are worn over the face or on the head. Sometimes, a mask may be as large as a also be life-sized object. According to *The New International Webster's Student Dictionary of the English Language* (Landau, 2000: 442), the word mask means '1. A cover or disguise for the features; 2. A protective appliance for the face or head; 3. Anything used to disguise or dissimilate; 4. A likeness of a face cast in plaster, clay, etc.; 5. An elaborate dramatic presentation with music, fanciful costumes, etc. and actors masked as allegorical or mythological subjects; also the text or music for it; 6. Masquerade; 7. An artificial covering for the face, used esp. by Greek and Roman actors'. The description of mask in the *New Encyclopedia Britannica* (1991: 910) aptly brings out the sense in which it has been used in this study. According to this encyclopedia, 'Mask, type of disguise, commonly an object worn over or in front of the face to hide the identity of the wearer. The features of the mask not only conceal those of the wearer, but also project the image of another personality or being. This dual function is a basic characteristic of mask'.

Masks are found to have been used in different parts of the world right from earliest ages in the history of mankind. Pani (1986: 1) writes,

> Nobody knows where and when mask originated. It seems probable that deep in the prehistoric past each primitive society developed its own masks to minimize the feeling of vulnerability. At the time scientific reason did not develop to explain the various phenomena of nature to which the primitive man was helplessly exposed. He, therefore, felt highly insecure and vulnerable. He could see that the forces of nature, which control him are basically of two kinds: the benevolent, and the malevolent. The former, he thought, are the acts of the gods whereas the latter, that of the demons and evil spirits. Thus he started creating myths and desperately tried to materialize these supernatural powers so that, through appropriate rituals which are but enactments of myths, the gods could be pleased and the evil spirits appeased. As a result, from his mythmaking faculty were born many idols, images and icons. And mask was born as a special kind of icon.

The chief motivation for making mask is probably to satisfy the magico-religious need of the primitive people. In their day to day life, they had to face a good number of hindrances like scarcity of food material, disease and death, natural calamities, etc. which they intended to overcome by wearing masks. The oldest evidence of the use of mask were encountered in the walls of cave and rock shelters during the Upper Palaeolithic period. Most of those were the paintings of hunters who were seen to cover their faces with animal masks. Even after achieving the higher culture and economy, the tradition of mask persisted in the human society. Even today it is not possible for men to fully control the nature; uncertainty still looms large on the life of human beings. To overcome such situations men wear masks, and through this they try to achieve happiness and prosperity by warding off the uncertainty of life. Although mask assumes various forms, the principal aim of the people is to get strength and prosperity by wearing masks. It is believed that by wearing animal mask, one can acquire the strength of that animal. Although both malevolent and benevolent mask are common in different societies, the principal function of masks is to ensure the cultural existence of men.

Laude (1971: 142) observes,

> The masks protects. Indeed, should the vital force liberated at the time of death be allowed to wander, it would harass the living and would disturb composure. Trapped in the mask, it is controlled, one might

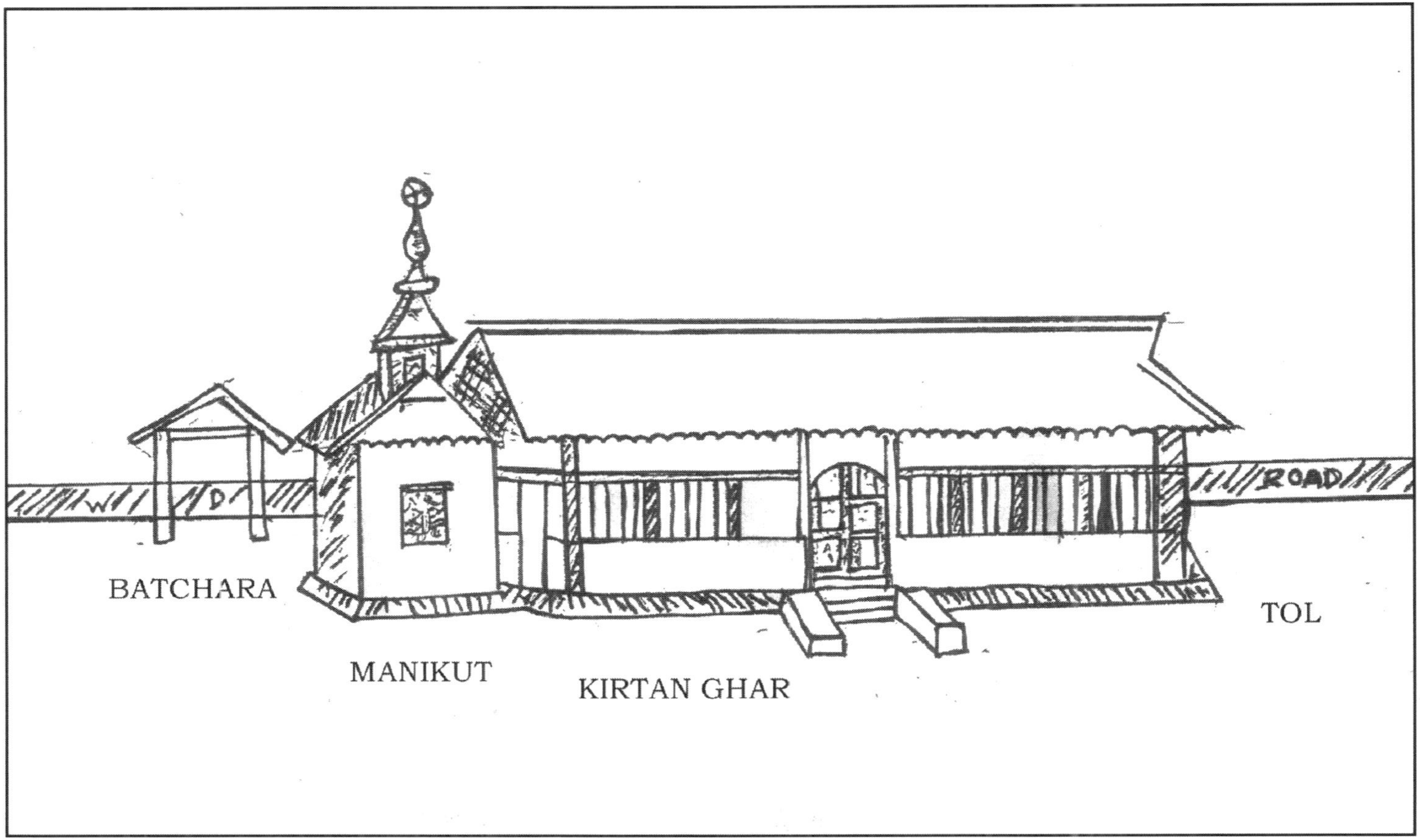

Fig. 1. A sketch of the Natun Chamaguri Satra.

say exploited, and then redistributed for the benefit of the collectivity. But the mask also safeguards the dancer who during the ceremony, must be protected from the influence of the instrument he manipulated.

In fact, humanity has travelled a long way and has undergone transformation, and man has become civilized and more objective in his outlook; but some elements of primitive psychology still exist him in the form of seen and unseen fear for the unknown even in the highly developed society. This is best expressed by the use of masks in different cultures. Though masks are as varied as the makers' imagination, beliefs and needs, they reflect the artistic and religious devotion of those who made them since the earliest time. The forms of masks have changed as the centre of which they had been a part, but their intrinsic value have remained the same, and thus time gets captured in the mask.

We look at the mask as a means of escaping from the reality of daily life to have an experience of participating in multifarious life in the universe. The wearer of a mask can sail out in the world of ecstasy; he can turn into a spirit, an animal, a demon, or a god that the mask depicts. As a social being, man lives in a community of similar individuals with whom he comes in contact constantly in the way of direct or indirect competition. He is equal to all in the sphere of socio-economic life, but his sub-conscious mind wants him to be distinguished and he is transformed into a character, to instill the fear among others. He does so to earn reverence and respect from others, at least for some time, on certain occasions. This he achieves through masks, because when a man wears a mask, he is transformed into the character of the mask.

The Natun (new) Chamaguri Satra is a renowned Vaishnavite monastery of Majuli, which has a long and rich tradition of mask making. In fact, this *satra* (Vaishnavite monastery), which is a bifurcation from the Chamaguri Satra (monastery), at present known as Prachin (old) Chamaguri Satra, continued the mask making tradition of its parent *satra*. Besides, there are two other *satras* in Majuli, viz., Alengi Narasimha Satra and Bihimpur Satra, which are also well known for their mask making tradition. The craft of mask making was closely linked with the rise and development of Vaishnavism in Assam. From the beginning, mask has been an integral part of ritualistic performances of the *satras*, *namghars* (village prayer house), and in other Vaishnavite community gatherings. The masks used in those occasions are generally made in the *satras*, and they had always been different and distinct from those of the other places of India. Even the masks of Assam, which are not associated with Vaishnavism, are conspicuously different from the Vaishnavite masks. These Vaishnavite masks are treated as animate objects, and the persons who wear these, and also the people who are associated with them, hold these masks in great reverence. The ingredients used in making these masks and their making process are way different from those of other parts of India. Moreover, these masks possess superb aesthetic beauty, and have socio-cultural, religious, theatrical, and other value. The present study on masks is confined mainly to those of Natun Chamaguri Satra of Majuli.

North-East India comprises seven states, viz., Arunachal Pradesh, Assam, Manipur, Meghalaya, Mizoram, Nagaland,and Tripura, and the region is predominantly inhabited by different tribes. Out of the seven states, four states, viz., Arunachal Pradesh (68.8%), Meghalaya (86.1%), Mizoram (94.4%), and Nagaland (86.5%), have tribal population in majority. About a quarter of the region is covered by hilly terrains, and another quarter is made up of the four plain areas, namely, the Brahmaputra Valley, the Barak Valley, the Manipur plateau, and the plain areas of Manipur. The entire region constitutes a geographical area of 2,55,083 sq. km of Indian territory having a population of 44.98 million (as per 2011 census). North-East India is the homeland of a good number of ethnic groups including as many as 209 scheduled tribes, almost half the number the communities so categorized in the whole of India. The seven states of North-East India constitute a single cultural zone. In the cultures of these seven states anyone can trace a good number of common cultural elements.

Assam is the gateway of North-East India and is the abode of a good number of communities—both tribals and non-tribals.

> Assam, located between tropical latitudes of 24.3° N and 28° N, and eastern longitudes of 89.5° E and 96.1°E, is the most populous state in North-East India. It is surrounded on three sides by hills and mountains. The rivers, Brahmaputra and Barak, in the north and south, respectively, carve out deep valleys, which represent the major part of the state. It is a transitional territory between South Asia and South-East Asia. The transition is reflected not only in the region's flora and fauna, but also in human types, languages, and cultures. Assam is surrounded by seven Indian states, which have such a strategic location. The state has an area of 78,438 sq. km representing 2.39 per cent of the Indian landmass

and a population of 22,414,322 (1991) accounting for 2.64 per cent of the total population of the country (Bhagabati et al., 2001: 1).

According to 2011 census, the total population of Assam is 31,169,272.

The present Assam was reconstituted after 1971 census. According to Puri (1968: 2), Professor of Indian History and Culture, National Academy of Administration, Mussoorie,

> The land with its flourishing passage with a romantic touch enveloping it, Assam as a name does not figure in Ancient Indian literature. The earlier inscriptions also do not mention it. The origin of the word remains a mystery. The ancient Assam was known as Pragjyotisha in *Mahabharata*, and as Kamrup in *Puranas* and *Tantras* (Gait, 2005: 10). The name Assam is Anglicized form of the Sanskrit word *'asama'* which means 'unparalleled' or 'peerless'. It is said that this was used to describe the invincible might of the Ahoms, who marched into this region in the thirteenth century from across the Patkai ranges. There is also other opinion about the origin of the name; this relates to the uneven terrain and the scenic grandeur 'without a peer', non-pereil of the country. It can therefore, be easily conjectured that the Sanskrit name, Asam and its Anglicized counterpart Assam, are not of distant origin (*National Family Health Survey*, 1995: 1-2).

In *Culture and Civilization of Assam*, Dutta (1958: 1) writes:

> Kamrupa or ancient Assam has been called a land of antiquarian surprises, unlike any other part of India, a land of profound interest to the historian, and the archaeologist, the linguist, and the Anthropologist. Here the most ancient and the most modern, the most up-to-date and most antiquated meet together in terms of perfect cordiality.

To explore Assam's (undivided) past and cultural synthesis, Das's (1967: 10) opinion deserves mention:

> The prehistoric past of Assam is still a matter of conjecture in the absence of adequate authentic information. No human remains of prehistoric time has yet been unearthed from any part of this region. Recently a few Paleolithic tools and a good number of Neolithic implements along with other finding have been reported.

This may throw some new light on the problem of prehistoric man and culture of Assam.

Till the recent past Assam was believed to be a land of black magic and sorcery. It was also believed that any alien person coming to Assam can become a sheep immediately under the spell of black magic practised by the autocthones. It should be noted here that the supreme *Saktipeeth* Kamakhya is situated in the Nilachal hills in the only city of Guwahati of Assam which is an immensely revered pilgrimage of the Hindus. Kamakhya, bountiful in natural resources in the fertile land of Assam, attracted people to this remote part of the country from distant past. In different periods groups of people came to Assam and settled here permanently marrying the local girls particularly the local Mongolian girls (Medhi, 2009).

Whatever might be the case of the prehistoric times, it is a known fact that from very distant past, Assam was like a highway connecting the rest of India with South-East Asia, through which passed people of diverse ethnic groups who differed in cultural entities and spoke different languages. Most of them not only left behind cultural remnants in this land, but also contributed towards the ethnic composition of the peoples. These have made Assam a place, where people of different cultural, linguistic, and ethnic groups live, each contributing towards the growth and development of a composite Assamese culture. This racial harmony was largely due to the gradual adaptation of Assamese which became the vehicle of expression of a composite people and also because of intimate contact among different ethnic groups throughout the centuries (Das, 1967: 10).

'Anthropologically speaking, almost nothing is known of Assam. For many centuries it occupied a peripherial position, both geographically and politically' (Cantlie, 1984: IX). It is very difficult to speak of the original inhabitants of Assam. Barkataki (1981: 4-5) supports this view and writes:

> All that we can say with certainty is that from about 200 BC there was a movement of population from the banks of the Hwangho and the Yang-tse-kiang in China to India through Assam, and these Mongolian people, along with others who migrated from northern Burma formed the bulk of the population of Assam.... About the time the Mongolian hordes were entering Assam from the north-east the Aryans started making their appearance in the Punjab from the north-west. Gradually they spread over the whole of northern India across the Gangetic plain, driving the local inhabitants, the Dravidians to the South. Eventually, some of the Aryans reached Assam in their eastward movement through Bihar and North Bengal. Judging however, by physiognomy, the strain of Aryan blood among the Assamese seems very thin.

1.2 THE ASSAMESE

The population of Assam by and large is Mongolian; fusion took place here between the cultures of Aryan and Mongolian. It is pertinent to note here that the Assamese are one of the principal inhabitants of Assam; their main concentration is found in the Brahmaputra valley of the state. Assamese is the principal language of Assam, and besides the Brahmaputra valley, in almost all the parts of the state it is accepted as the connecting language among different ethnic groups having different pristine languages and cultures. 'The modern Indian languages descended from Sanskrit and therefore called Indo-Aryan languages which are Hindi-Urdu. Bengali, Marathi, Gujrati, Oriya, Assamese, Rajasthani (vaiation of Hindi), Punjabi, Sindhi, Pashto, and Kashmiri' (Barua, 1965: 11). 'Assamese is a composite language into which words of both Indo-Aryan and Indo-Chinese origin have made their way. Over and above this, other pre-Aryan and non-Aryan influences are also discernable, not only loan wards, but also in point of grammar, syntax, and pronunciation' (Barua, 1965: 15).

Assamese language had to pass through different stages of development at different times, following which acquired the present form in the process of formation and development. This language has incorporated in it good number of words from different languages like Austric, Dravidian, Tibeto-Burman, Arabic, English, Parsi, etc. which have enriched the Assamese vocabulary. Theoretically, whoever speaks Assamese language is an Assamese; in this sense it includes the Bangladeshis and tea garden workers also. In practice, however, not all those Assamese-speaking communities are considered to be the Assamese. In broader sense, the term Assamese is sometimes used to refer to those who are the inhabitants of Assam; in this sense also it includes all the non-Assamese communities inhabited in the state. Generally, however, the term is used to denote the indigenous and long settled inhabitants of the state, who are recognized as Assamese, not only in language, but also in culture and way of life.

At the time of 2011 census there were 26,395 inhabited villages in Assam with an average population of over 500 people. However, the cadastral village is not a social unit. In practice, the inhabitants of a village are united on the basis of the membership of local centre of devotional worship, particularly to a *namghar*. The members of a particular *namghar, masjid, gurdwara,* etc. describe themselves as *raij*

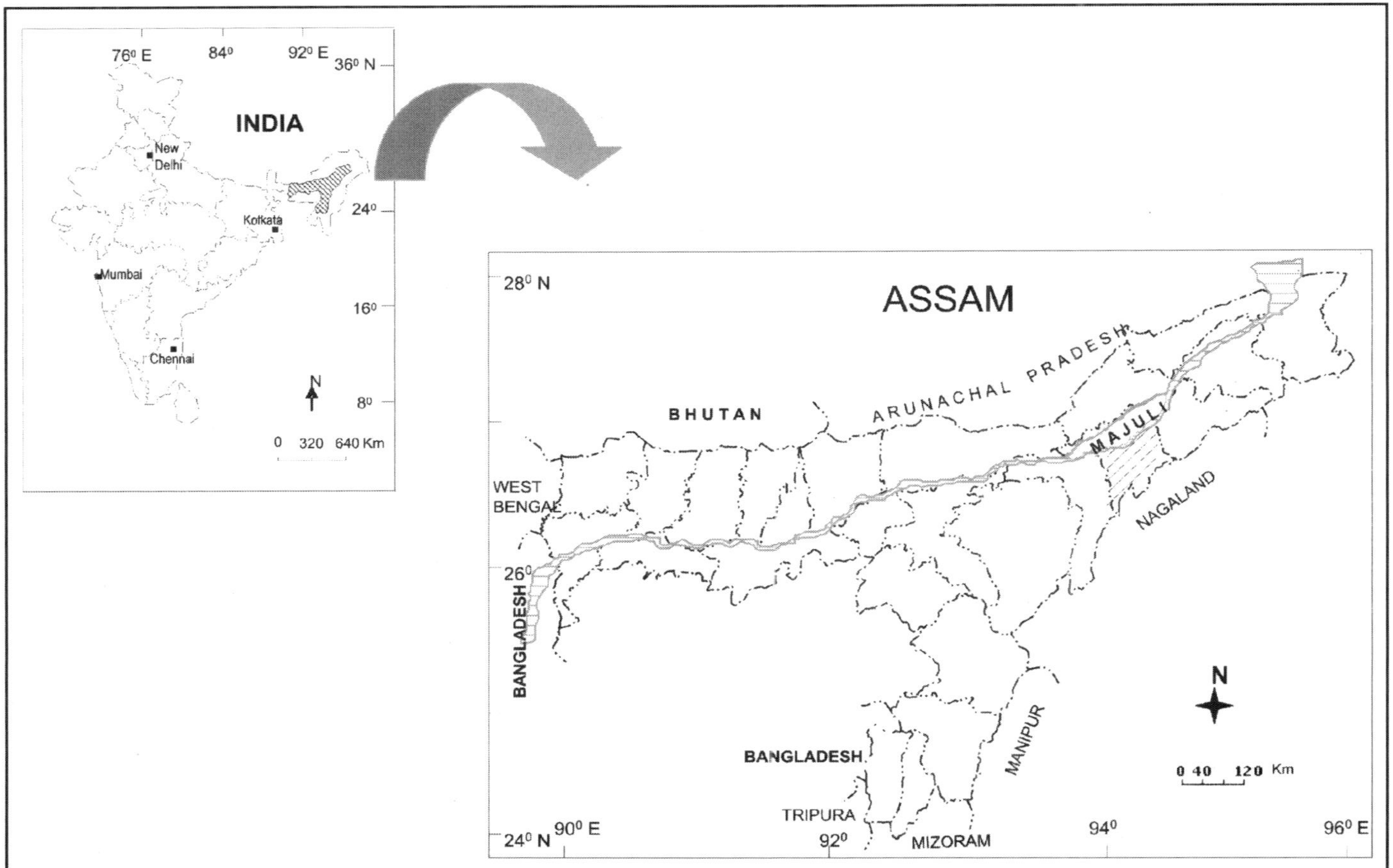

Fig. 2. Map of India showing the location of Assam.

(group of a community). *Namghar* may be of single caste or multi caste; generally each Assamese village possesses one or more *namghars*. It should be noted here that an Assamese village is geographically not a well-defined unit, and it is difficult to separate physically an Assamese village from the surrounding other villages.

The overwhelming majority of the Assamese are rural inhabitants, and agriculture is their mainstay. They practise wet cultivation and their principal crop is paddy. Generally, they cultivate two varieties of paddy: the summer paddy, and the winter paddy. They also cultivate mustard, sesame, sugarcane, black gram, jute, different varieties of vegetables, etc. Traditionally, the Assamese people built their houses almost at the centre of the homestead compound keeping a frontyard (*ag-chotal*) and a backyard (*pach-chotal*). The courtyard (*chotal)* is an indispensable part of the Assamese residential unit where most of mundane duties are carried out. In a typical dwelling unit, a cluster of houses is found. Different houses are used for different purposes like sleeping, cooking, paddy storing, cow keeping, and so on. Traditionally, the houses are made of wood, bamboo, thatch, cane, reed, etc. The houses have raised rectangular plinths with wooden or bamboo posts supporting the thatched roofs and reed or split bamboo walls. The walls are plastered with mud mixed with cow dung. At present these houses are replaced by Assam type houses and R.C.C. buildings.

Boiled rice is the staple food of the Assamese. Irrespective of caste and creed, the Assamese are non-vegetarian, and consume fish, egg, meat, etc. along with rice. However, among different religious groups, there are some taboos on food. They usually prepare a good number of snacks from rice. In all rituals of the Assamese rice or items prepared from rice is indispensable. Tea and betel nut are an integral part of the Assamese food. Tea is taken with or without luncheon. Areca nut with betel vine leaves, and with or without a pinch of lime, is taken by the Assamese people irrespective of age, sex, social status at any time. These two items are also used by them to entertain guests. Assamese utensils, which are used for serving different items of food, are spectacularly different from that of the other parts of India. With regard to dress and ornaments also, the Assamese people are noticeable.

Traditionally, each of the Assamese girl is a skilled weaver, and till date weaving is a living tradition in Assam. The pristine dress of a man is a *dhuti* (an unsewn piece of long cloth) and a *chola* (shirt). An unsewn white piece of cloth with thin coloured borders about 4.5 mt, called *dhuti,* is used by the adult male to cover the lower part of his body. The elderly women wear *mekhela,* a kind of skirt, which covers their body from waist to heels. To cover the upper part of the body a woman wears a blouse, over which a *chadar,* i.e., a long unsewn piece of cloth about 2.75 mt in length is used as a wrapper. Along with the pristine dress and ornaments, nowadays the Assamese women wear non- traditional dress and ornaments also.

The population of Assam by and large is Mongolian; but there has been fusion of Mongolian life ways with Aryan culture. Biswas and Ojah (2002: 105-106) write,

> Assam has been the meeting place of two great world's civilizations, Indian and Chinese. It has been receiving successive waves of migration at different times from different directions (that is China, India, Burma, and Tibet) since ancient times which made the population of Assam diverse with multiplicity of race, religion, and culture.... The interaction of various cultures and civilization produced a distinctive synthesis of Assam's culture and society.

In Assam, no rigid caste system is found and untouchability is unheard here. Hamilton in his book entitled *An Account of Assam* (1940: 51-57) has made a list of the castes and tribes of Assam and observes,

> There are no confectioners, no butchers, no tailors (1940: 63). Although there are a good number of castes occupying different position in caste hierarchy of Assam, but due to the flaccidity in the system the castes of Assam can broadly be divided into two categories only – the Brahmins, and non-Brahmins. Except for certain communities such as the Kaibartas, which are classed as 'scheduled caste', there are free intercourse and intermarriage amongst the non-Brahmin communities, such as Kalitas of Aryan extraction, and the Keots, who are of Mongolian origin. This significant feature of Assamese society can possibly be ascribed to the predominantly Mongolian strain in the composition of the people.

This view of Barkataki is supported by many scholars. In *The Census of India* (1931: 211), Mullan comments,

> Caste in the Assam Valley is not as elsewhere, chiefly a functional division; it is really a racial division and functional castes are very few. This is partly due to the fact that many tasks, which in other parts of India are assigned to particular castes, are carried out in Assam by individual households. Men and woman wash their own clothes

without the help of a caste washer man. Excrement is left on the ground so there is no need of a caste of sweepers. Men (except the Brahmans) shave themselves and cut their hair without the help of Barbers. Bamboo work is not caste bound and may be undertaken by anyone with the necessary skill. Both men and women can catch fish without objection for household consumption, though not for sale. Further, the specialist caste that exist (potters, blacksmiths, goldsmiths, fishermen, weavers, silk-rearers, etc.) are not tied as dependent serving families to individual land owning households but sell their wares, either at a fixed price within their village or for what they can get in market. Most are part time cultivators.

Stack (1981: 63) comments that

perhaps the higher level of respectability on which the lower caste generally stand in Assam may be explained partly by the circumstances of a country where land is abundant, and where nobody is restricted to any degrading occupation as the only available means of earning his bread.

In the eyes of different non-Assamese persons, the Assamese have acquired notable positions. A Swedish lady, Sigrid Hydari, wife of the first Indian Governor of Assam, Sir Akbar Hydari, had made some interesting observations on the character of the Assamese people:

The Assamese possesses in my eyes, the virtue and defects of the born aristocrate. His natural dignity rarely deserts him in any crisis, big or small. He will not bestir himself unduely for the sake of added lucre. An 'elegant self-sufficiency' is his motto ... we found the Assamese courteous and friendly on approach, but he did not intrude himself. He always showed his respect in silence, not by shouting and hand-waving.

As regards Assamese women, I cannot resist the temptation of quoting the following remarks of Mahatma Gandhi made in *Young India* (1921). 'And, of course, I fell in love with the women of Assam as soon as I learnt that they are accomplished weavers .... And to me it is a sign of very high culture to see the Assamese women and girls little or no jewellery. They are like women all over India, shy and modest with extremely refined and open faces.

To these might be added the observations of the scholar Governor Sri Sriprakash to complete the picture:

The Assamese proper is a simple agriculturist who weaves his own cloth and grows his own food. He is a proud and sensitive person

> wedded to tradition and glorying in his history, his legend and his isolation. The women know both the domestic arts of spinning and weaving, and the fine arts of dancing and singing. Wrapped in a mantle of modesty, that so becomes them, they go about their work with free and assured steps that truly make them the ideal representative of their sex (cited in Barkataki, 1981: 17-18).

The Assamese recognized two categories of kin comprehended in the term *mitir* or *mitra* and *kutum* or *kutumba,* i.e., affines and agnates, respectively. The *kutum* is usually identified with the agnatic line or house (*bamgsa*), and *bamgsa* connected by marriage becomes affines to one another. There are two agnatic groups: the descent group, and the family (*pariyal*). The descent group is identified in the male line from a common ancestor within seven generations. Some opine that the descent group lasts forever and, therefore, no marriage should take place as long as any connection can be traced; however, in practice only a few men can name their great grandfather. In Assam, commensality is seen as the defining criterion of a family. In every household there is one kitchen and a husking lever (*dhenki*). Division of joint family is understood as eating separately, and in course of time it will be followed by constructing a separate residential unit, and the division of land and property. Affinity is conceived in terms of the transformation of woman from one descent group to another, both physically and ritually. Affinal ties usually persist for two generations. A son-in-law is required to visit his wife's parents at least two times a year at the local seasonal festivals, i.e., during Bohag Bihu (festival of merry-making during March-April), and in Magh Bihu (festival of feasting performed during December-January), and his children will visit their mother's father's house where their maternal uncle lives. Gradually, these ties lapse and only a few men know the natal village of their father's mother. All the descent groups to whom a daughter has been given, or from whom a daughter-in-law has been taken are considered affines.

Marriage is prohibited within the descent group for seven or nine generations reckoned by patrilineal descent from a common male ancestor. Marriage is also prohibited with a daughter's line (*jiyari bamgsa*) consisting of his relatives by cognitive descent from a common ancestor within five generations. However, in practice, marriages take place when the old people can no longer trace any relationship with the would-be bride's family. Possession of a common clan (*gotra)* name is also a bar to marriage. A *gotra* takes its name from a hermit of ancient time, and membership in decades putative patrilineal descent from the offspring or disciple who shared his grazing ground. In practice, however, the clan system limits the choice of spouse only in the case of Brahmans and perhaps a few Kayastha families, as almost all the other castes are members of Kashyapa clan within which marriage is allowed. Non-Brahman castes require a clan name only for the performance of some Vedic rites, and if a man does not know his clan, the priest will assign him to Kashyapa clan. One of the notable features of Assamese marriage is the absence of dowry. Marriage by negotiation and elopement are common among the Assamese people.

The principal festival of Assam is Bihu, which is is a seasonal festival observed in the month of *Bohag, Kati* (September-October), and *Magh.* These are known as Bohag Bihu or *Rongali* Bihu, Kati Bihu or *Kangali* Bihu (poor Bihu), and Magh Bihu or *Bhogali* Bihu. Among these three Bohag Bihu is the principal one, and observed with merry making and feasting by all the Assamese people irrespective of caste and creed. Besides the Bihus, the Assamese people observe many festivals principally integral to religion and agriculture.

1.3 MAJULI

In Assam there are 27 districts and Jorhat district is one of them. It is pertinent to note here that the study area, i.e., Majuli island, is situated in the said district. Majuli is the largest river island of Assam, which is situated in the upper reaches of the river Brahmaputra within the latitude of 26°45′ N – 27°12′ N and longitude of 93°39′E - 94°35′ E with mean height of 84.5 mt above mean sea level. It should be noted here that almost all the people of Assam and many others believe that Majuli is the largest fresh water island of the world. However, this belief is not true because Ilha Do Bananal of Amazon river of Brazil is the largest river island of the world. The Araguaia is a tributary of the Amazon river, and the Ilha Do Bananal is situated amidst two rivulets, i.e., Javes and Riozinho of Aragusia. The Ilha Do Bananal is extended from 10°S latitude to 13°15′ south latitude, and 49°44′ W longitude to 51°33′ W longitude. The mean height of the island is in between 171 mt to 239 mt. The island is spread across 11,000 sq. km; in length it is 320 km and the maximum breadth is 55 km. The mean height of Majuli is 84.5 mt above mean sea level. The length of Majuli is 54 km and the breadth of

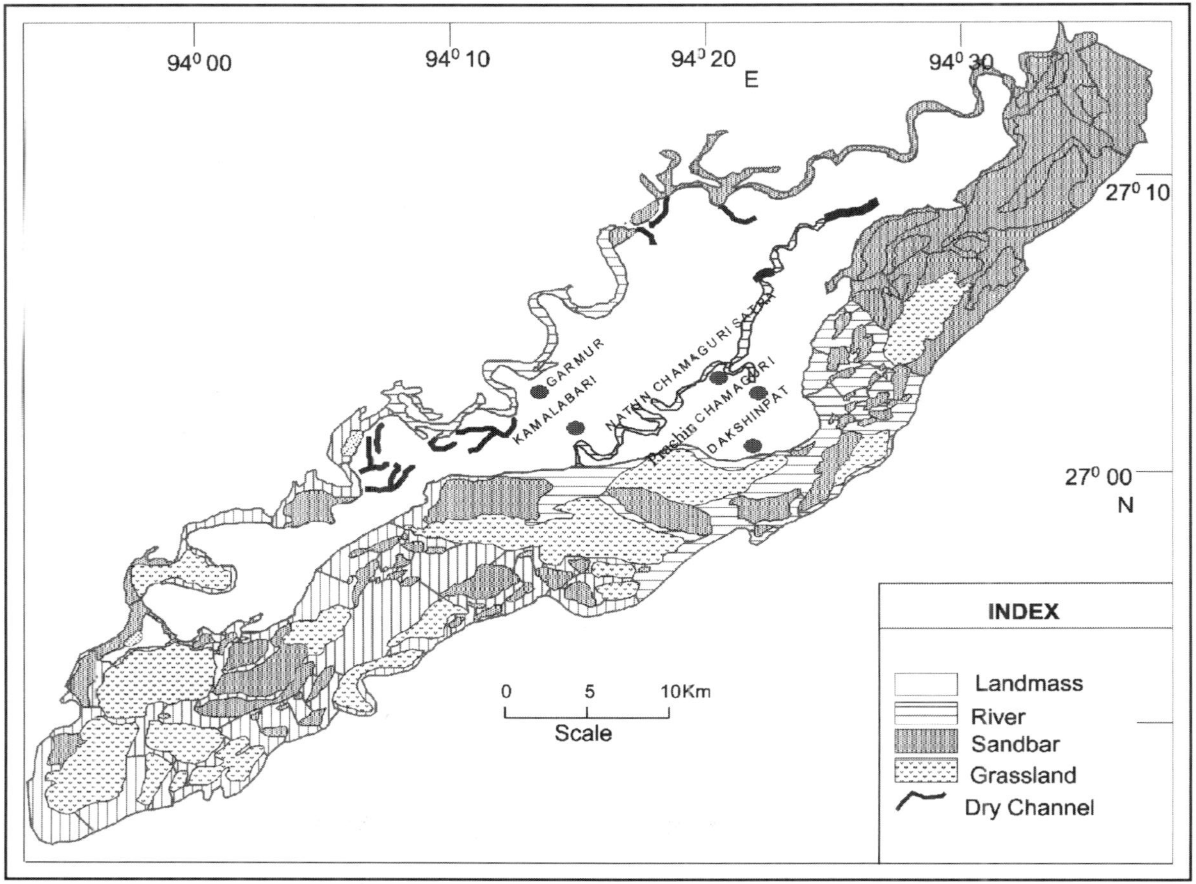

Fig. 3. Map of Majuli showing the Prachin Chamaguri Satra and the Natun Chamaguri Satra

it is only 15 km. Due to relentless erosion, the area of Majuli has been frequently changing and at present its area is 30,584.00 hectares only. Due to the continuous erosion, the very existence of Majuli is under threat. Since the great earthquake of 1950, it is facing substantial erosion which has became acute after 1974. In the past half century, about 1/3rd of the landmass of Majuli has been eroded. Floods of Brahmaputra River create havoc annually in the island.

Majuli is the epitome of natural and cultural heritage of Assam, and attempt has been made to preserved the island under the aegis of UNESCO as a world heritage site. As already mentioned, Majuli lies in Jorhat district. The name Jorhat means a 'pair of market places', *hat* means a 'weekly market', and *jor* means 'a pair'. During the 18th century there were two important weekly markets in Jorhat district on either side of the Bhogdoi River, i.e., Macharhat and Chowkihat, from which the place acquired its name. The Ahom king Gaurinath Singha (1780-1795) shifted the capital of his kingdom from Sivasagar, erstwhile Rangpur, to Jorhat.

Jorhat was a flourishing commercial town but destroyed by a series of Burmese invasion since 1817 till the arrival of British force in 1824 under the leadership of David Scott and Captain Richard. The British rule helped to revive this historical town. At present the district spreading over 2851 sq km with a population of 10, 922, 56 (2011 census), density of 383 persons per sq km with a sex ratio 933. The district has 88,665 scheduled caste and 1, 39,971 scheduled tribe population, and 8.12 per cent and 12.81 per cent of the total population, respectively. Jorhat has 848 revenue villages among which 763 are inhabited and 85 are uninhabited. The river Brahmaputra forms one of the largest riverine island of the world , Majuli , on the north of the district, spreading over 1254.12 sq km with a population of about 1,67,304 (2011 census; 85566 males and 81738 females) , of a density of 134.4 persons per sq km . Majuli is a sub-division where there are 248 revenue villages among which 192 are inhabited and 56 are uninhabited. The mean annual rainfall of Majuli is 2029 mm. Continuous erosion has reducing the size of the island and at present total area of Majuli is 1254.12 hectors. The tribal population like the Mishing, the Deoris, etc. formed 46.38 per cent of the total population of Majuli.

The Brahmaputra riverine tract with its peculiar geo-environmental elements forms a distinctive zone so far as the bio-diversity of Majuli is concerned. This is the tract through which a wave of the south-west monsoon moves eastward that causes heavy rain in the foothills of the Himalayas and the Barail range.It should be mentioned here that the said tract can be considered as the base line from which variations in the biotic environment occur gradually towards the Himalayas on the north and Meghalaya and Karbi plateau on the south. The water bodies in the tract along with their conspicuously rich aquatic resources act as the nucleus of attraction for a large number of animals and birds, particularly during the winter season, adding additional significance in the ecosystem of North-East India. High amount of rainfall, very high moisture in soil during the summer, and the flat nature of plain favour the growth of a good number of evergreen, semi-evergreen, and deciduous trees, a wide variety of marsh vegetation, bamboos, grasses, canes, etc. Although growing pressure of population on the island has created severe degradation of the natural environment including flora, the luxurious growth of the following vegetations are conspicuous in the island: *ajar* (*Lagerstroemis flos-reginae*), *amlakhi* (*Texminatia chebula*), *anhat* (*Ficus religiosa*), *arjuna* (*Termintia arjuan*), *dimaru* (*Ficus glomerata*), *hollock* (*Bischofla javanica*), Indian almond tree (*Baringtonia acutangula*), *jamu Eugenia jambolana*), *kadam* (*Anthocephalus cadamba*), *khair* (*Acacia catechu*), *neem* (*Azadirachta indica*), *ou tenga* (*Dellenia indica*), *simalu* (*Bombax ceiba*), *siris / koroi* (*Albizzia procera*), etc. Among the deciduous trees *ajar* and *simalu*, which grow luxuriantly up to a height of 35 meters, are of great importance.

There are more than 60 wet lands in Majuli of varying size and depth, which include Oudubi, Bhereki, Chakuli, Dubaritali, Kharikata, Kharkhari, etc. These water bodies are full of different kinds of aquatic plants. Due to the lack of continuous forest belt in Majuli, large mammals are rarely seen here. A few wild water buffaloes are found in the island. Other animals include barking deer (*Muntiacus muntjak*), Chinese pangolin (*Manis pentadactyla*), eastern mole (*Talpa micrura*), Indian grey mongoose (*Herpestes Edwardsii*), rhesus monkey (*Macaca mulatta*), river dolphin (*platanista gangutica*), bat (*Scotophilus heathis*), civet (Viverricula *indica*), etc. The island of Majuli is also rich in aves, amphibians, and reptiles. There are a good number of riverine islands (*char*) adjacent to current flow which is inundated in floods where different kinds of local and migratory birds are seen.

The mainstay of the people is agriculture. Majuli has a rich and spectacular agricultural tradition of growing as many as a hundred different varieties of paddy; the inhabitants also cultivate both Kharif and Rabi crops. The other occupation of the people are bamboo and cane craft, boat making, cattle farming, handloom, horticulture, pottery, sericulture, etc. Majuli has been the abode of Assamese Vaishnavite culture with great potential for spiritual and eco-tourism.

Majuli is famous for the great Vaishnavite saint and social reformer Sankaradeva (1449–1568), who visited the island in the early sixteenth century. Sankaradeva propagated a form of Vaishnavism which was simpler and more accessible than the Hinduism indispensably related to many rites and rituals of that time. Sankaradeva stressed in doing the regular duties of people, and along with that one should pray the only God, Lord Vishnu for the well-being of the self and the community. The cult propagated by Sankaradeva was based on the worshipping of Lord Vishnu. Medhi (2008: 90-91) writes:

> Vishnu is the supreme being for the Vaishnavas, his worshippers, and they believe that all things emanate from the deity. Vishnu, The preserver and the restore has enormous popularity throughout India, whose appeasement invariably emits splendour and gaiety. Vishnu has one thousand names (*sahasra nama)*, among which eight are treated as principal names, these are: Achyuta (unfallen, imperishable), Kesava (the hairy, the radiant), Janardana (whom men worship), Narayana (who moves in water), Vishnu (who pervades), Satya (the truth), Hamsa (the graceful gaiter), and Hari (Lord of sense organs). It is immensely believed by the devotees of Vishnu that, who wholeheartedly utters these names, his or her desires are fulfilled. Besides these, Vishnu has many other popular names like Ananta (the endless), Chakradhara / Cakrapani (who holds a quoit named Sudarsana), Caturbhuja (the four handed), Damodara (tied with rope around the belly), Govinda / Gopala (the cowherd), Jalasayina (who sleeps on water), Lakshmipati (consort of goddess Lakshmi), Madhusudana (destroyer of the demon Madhu), Mukunda (the deliverer), Murari (the foe of the demon Mura), Panchayudha (armed with five weapons), Padmanava (whose navel is like a lotus), Pitambara (garbed in yellow coloured cloth), Purusottoma (the best of men), Sarangadhara / Sarangapani (who holds the bow named saranga), Sridhara (the handsome one), Vaikunthanatha / Vaikunthapati (Lord of heaven, i.e., *Vaikuntha*), and so on. Vishnu has been manifested to the world in ten principal incarnations (*avatara*) taking a variety of forms like fish (*matchya*), tortoise *(kurma*), man-lion (*nara-simha*), etc. In course of time the number of these incarnations

have been increased to twenty four. Lord Vishnu took those forms to end some evils in the world. While all these incarnations are revered by the Hindus, Rama and Krishna, especially Krishna, is greatly honoured as the full incarnation (*purna avatara*) of Vishnu. He is the most cherished mythological hero of India, and believed to be the direct manifestation of Vishnu himself. The followers of Vaishnavism, who believe only in one God Vishnu, are known as the Vaishnava. Vishnu is the supreme being for the Vaishnavas, his worshippers, and they believe all things emanate from the deity. Vishnu, the preserver and the restorer has enormous popularity through India whose appeasement invariably emits splendour and gaiety....

The Neo-Vaishnavite movement initiated by Sankaradeva (1449-1568) in Assam was a part of the larger pan-Indian resurgence of Bhakti (unflinching devotion) in medieval India that spanned nearly a little over five centuries from the devotional cult of Alvars in Tamilnadu to the teaching of Ramanuja, Nimbarka, Madhavacharyya, Vallabhacharyya, Chaitanya, Kabir, Guru Nanak and others. While it was basically a reaction against the excess of sacerdotal religion, the spirit of new ideas manifested itself in an overall social change almost unprecedented in its scale in the history of Assam. Sankaradeva was an extraordinarily gifted man, widely travelled, well versed in traditional Sanskrit learning, poet, playwright and musician par excellence (Neog, 1988: 1).

The doctrine propounded by Sankardeva proved to be a great unifying force in Assam and initiated by concept of oneness among the people irrespective of caste and creed in this part of land. The caste Hindus, different tribal groups, even the Muslims were brought in the universe of Neo-Vaishnavism and had accelerated the process of integration among the diverse groups of Assam. (Medhi, 2009).

In the noteworthy book entitled *The Place of Assam in the History and Civilization of India*, Chatterjee writes:

> He gave to Assam a new discipline of faith..... and helped Assam to break away with a past with its complicated esoteric doctrine and its unmeaning practices and gave to the people something simple and straight forward divested of all questionable associations or implications. He was the greatest builder of Assam bringing in a purer spiritual life, and although circumstances prevented his influence from being spread into other part of India, as a religious leader he is unquestionably one of the greatest India has produced and he deserved to be mentioned with Sankaracharyya, Ramanujacharyya, Basavappa, Ramananda, Kabir, Chaitanya, Mira Bai, Guru Nanak and Tulsidasa.

> He was truly the medium through whom the spiritual light of medieval India as a whole shown up upon the life of Assam (cited in Neog, 1988: 1).

It should be noted here that Vaishnavism of Assam was moulded in accordance with the social environment of that time, for which the simple and illiterate people of Assam were greatly attracted to that religion. Sarma (1999: 1-2) writes:

> The new cult thus moulded according to the local circumstance was popularly known as the *Mahapurusiya-dharma*. The real name of the cult was *Ekasaranadharma* or the religion of supreme surrender to one God, viz. Visnu-Krasna. The term Mahapurusiya, generally applied to mean Sankaradeva. He was known to his followers as Mahapurusa (the great being) and therefore the religion propagated by him came to be known as the *Mahapurusiya-dharma*. But another explanation of the designation Mahapurusiya-dharma may be suggested. The term Mahapurusa is also an epithet of God Narayana. In a few verses of Bhagavata purana (II/1/10, XI/5/33) it has been used in the above sense. Sukadeva, the expounder or the *Bhagvata-purana*, addressed Pariksita as a Mahapaurusika, i.e., a devotee of Mahapurusa. As the Vaisnava cult of Assam enjoins the worship of Narayana only, the cult probably came to be known as the Mahapurusiya-dharma, i.e. the cult of Mahapurusa.

To propagate the faith, Sankaradeva adopted various means among which mention may be made of two religious institutions: *namghar* (the village-level prayer house), and *satra* (the Vaishnavite monastery), which proved to be very effective. Assamese Vaishnavism is institutionalized in *namghar* at the village level and in each Hindu village of Assam there is one or more *namghar* where the village members pray usually forming congregation (*samuha, raij*). *Namghar* is a simple house which is divided into two parts—a small room and a hall. The room is known as *manikut* (broadly, a chapel), where one to five prescribed scriptures, i.e., *Kirtana, Dasama, Namghosa, Gunamala*, and *Bhakti Ratnavali*, are placed in the *thapana* (a decorative wooden structure) or *Guru asana* (seat of the *Guru)*. The hall is generally devoid of walls, where the regular and occasional congregation are held to propitiate Lord Vishnu/Krishna. Different annual and occasional prayers are performed forming different groups in different times in the *namghar*. Usually nobody resides in a *namghar*. Each *namghar* is affiliated to a *satra*.

The word *satra* is a corrupt form of the Sanskrit word *sattra*. In Sanskrit literature, the word has been used in two senses. Firstly, in the sense of an alms-house, and secondly in the sense of a sacrifice lasting from a few days to a year or more. The term *satra* literally means *adhivesana* (an assembly), *homa* or *jangya* (sacred fire), or *nivasa* (abode). There are around 650 *satras* in Assam. The *satras* contribute to a significant part of Vaishnavite literature, art, culture, and spiritual elevation. To quote Sarma (1999: 1):

> The most notable characteristic of the Vaishnavism of Assam is the *satra* institution through which the faith was propagated and stabilized. It may be monastic as well as semi-monastic in form. The former type resemble to a certain extent to the Buddhist monasteries of ancient times, and the *maths* of medieval age. But the importance of the institution lies in the fact that it is intimately connected with the Assamese society and it has become a part and parcel of Assamese life. Contribution of this institution towards the spread of Vaishnavism in particular and the cultural development of Assam in general, are indeed great. The high percentage of people professing Vaishnavism in Assam is accountable to the activities of this institution during the last four centuries of the Christian era. It is because of the evangelical activities of this institution that many non-Aryan tribes today profess Vaishnavism in Assam.

1.4 ASPECTS OF *SATRA*

A *satra* is a residential unit where a Guru and some devotees (*bhaktas*) occupying different hierarchical positions live. From the structural angle, a *satra* is akin to a *namghar* except its huge structure. In four sides of the prayer house (*Kirtan-ghar, namghar*) of a typical *satra*, the residential houses of the devotees are constructed in straight lines. Such a residential line of the devotees are known as *hati*. The head of a *satra* is known as *satradhikar* (owner of the *satra*, the principal abbot) or *gosain* (god). All the *satras* of Assam are principally headed by persons belonging to two castes—Brahman and Kayastha. In some of the *satras*, the *satradhikars* and the *bhaktas* are celibates, while in some others they are allowed to marry. The celibate devotees are known as *kevaliya bhakta*.

Neog opines:

> The permanent organization of the devotional movement in Assam takes two forms: one is that of the village name house and the other is the *satra* system. A *satra* consists of a *guru* and the disciples initiated by

> him. Every Assamese Vaishnava prior to marriage journeys to his *satra* to take initiation from the Gosain who imparts to him the esoteric *mantras* of the sect. Therefore he required to live the life of a disciple who has dedicated himself to god and to support the *satra* by the payment of annual dues. These are estimated to be some 650 *satras* in Assam Valley. The head of the *satra,* who is termed the *satradhikar* ('owner of the satra') or *Gosain* ('god'), traces his spiritual genealogy by hereditary succession or by the link of initiation through his predecessors in office to the founder of his *satra,* and thence to the founder of his sub sect who was one of the disciples initiated by Shankaradeva, a Mahapurusa and incarnation of Vishnu (according to the Mahapurusia version of events). The lives of Shankaradeva and his immediate followers are recorded in an extensive biographical literature, which is said to date from the early half of the seventeenth century. The first four biographies, though not always in agreement, are held to be largely authoritative, while progressively less reliance is placed on the later works of the late seventeenth and early eighteenth centuries, by which time it had become an act of piety to model the career of the master on the episodes of Krishna's life as recounted in the *Bhagavata Purana* (cited in Cantlie, 1984: 152).

Sankaradeva established the first *satra*, the Dhuvahat Belguri, at Majuli to nurture and propagate his philosophy and practice of life. In the hey day of Sankaradeva, there were 65 *satras* in Assam, each with a good number of devotees or disciples and several thousand followers all over the state. The *satra* is a living tradition of Assam. At present there are around 22 *satras* at Majuli, some of which are still flourishing and others are in a dilapidated condition. It should be mentioned here that four *satras* (*chari satra*) are treated by the Assaemese Vaishnava as epitome of the local Vaishnavism. These satras are—Auniati, Dakshinpat, Gormur, and Kuruabahi. Among these four, the Kuruabahi is situated at Golaghat district and the remaining three are situated at Majuli, for which the Assamese people in general and the Assamese Vaishnavite in particular, revere Majuli as the supreme sacred place of Vaishnavism. According to the Vaishnavas of Assam, these four *satras* represent four hands or four weapons of Lord Vishnu. Lord Vishnu has four principal weapons, i.e., *sankha* (conch), *chakra* (quoit), *gada* (mace), and *padma* (lotus); these weapons are believed to be very powerful and effective. The Vaishnavas of the state believe that the said *satras* possess enormous spiritual power. Some opine that these four *satras* represent the four directions—north, south, east, and west.

1.5 THE VILLAGE SCENARIO

The village Natun Chamaguri is situated in the Majuli sub-division under the Bangaon outpost of the Jorhat district of Upper Assam. It is a component village of the Mekheli cadestral village. The total area of Mekheli Gaon is 318.64 hectare. There are four villages within the jurisdiction of Makheli Gaon; these are Dalani Chamaguri, Natun Chamaguri, Pukhuparia, and Mekheli Gaon. The Natun Chamaguri village is situated at a distance of about 8 km from Kamalabari police station. The village is a small one and roughly 2.5 km long and 2 km across. It is a multicaste village and is inhabited by people of three castes, viz., Kalita, Kayastha, and Koch.

In Assam, caste is not a functional division as elsewhere and caste of this state is principally a racial division. The Kalitas occupy a higher caste status in the sudra division of Assam. The Kalita caste is divided into many sub-castes: Kamar Kalita, Kumar Kalita, Dulia Kalita, Katani Kalita, Mali Kalita, Nat Kalita, Sonari Kalita, etc. and their traditional occupations are blacksmithery, pottery making, palanquin bearing, silk rearing, collecting flowers for temple, dancing in the temple, and gold smithery, respectively. Nowadays, most of the Kalitas are engaged in agriculture and in different urban occupations for their livelihood. The Kayastha is a caste whose traditional occupation was scribing and helping the zamindars. It should be noted here that Srimanta Sankaradeva, the founder of Vaishnavism in Assam, was a member of the Kayastha caste. In Assam, there are principally two divisions of the *satras;* one is headed by Brahmin *satradhikar,* while the other division is controlled by Kayastha *satradhikar.* The Koch is an agricultural caste supposed to have been originally formed as a result of conversion of the various tribal groups to Hinduism. Due to the tribe caste continuums the people from different tribes adopted Hinduism and they were all included in the Koch caste. Therefore, it is difficult to analyze the Koches as a single caste group. They are divided into a number of sub-groups according to their tribes of origin and time period of adopting Hinduism with distinct social, cultural, and religious background, and those act as powerful catalysts even after the inclusion in the same caste.

The Natun Chamaguri village is surrounded by Bankhowa Chuk and Deka Sanchowa in the north, Purani Chamaguri and Mudoi Chuk in the south, Bihimpur and Charingati Village in the west, and Bangaon and Mudoitali Village in the eastern side. The Natun Chamaguri Village

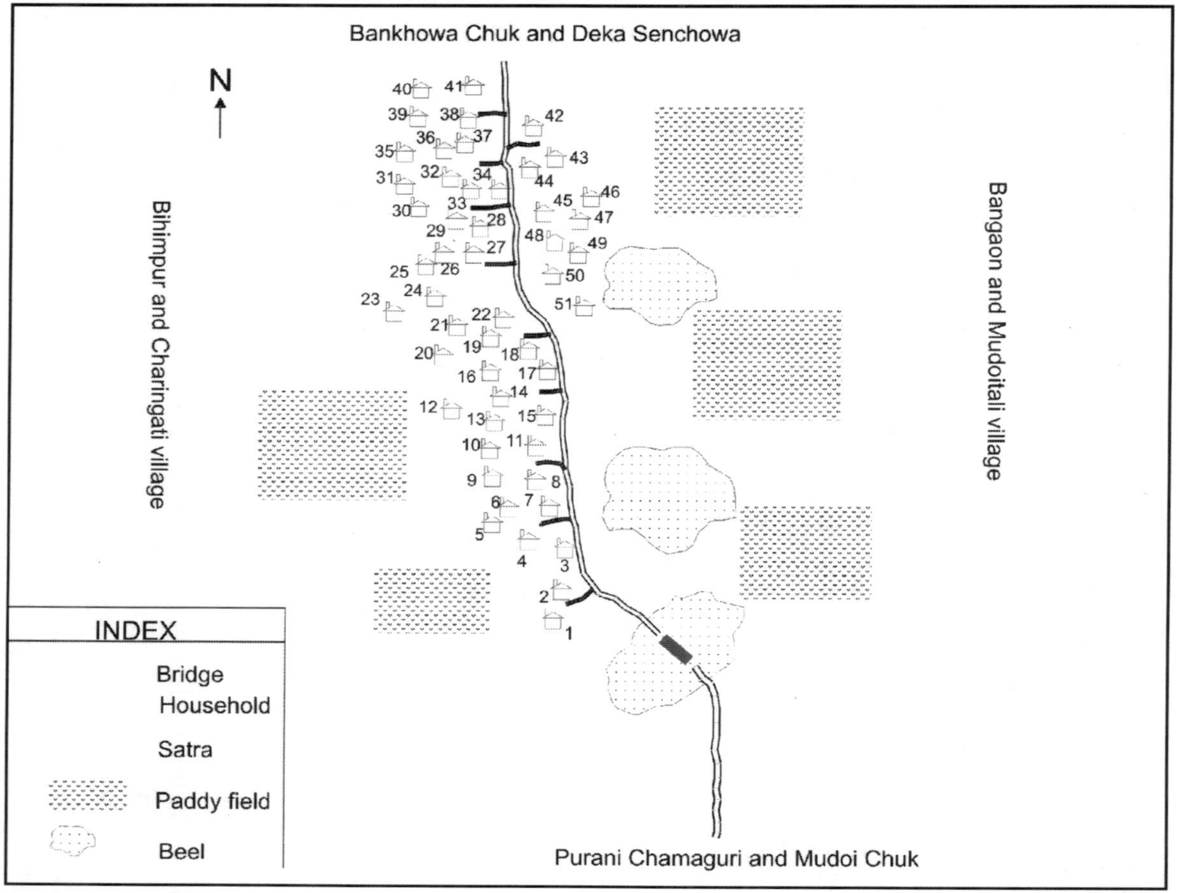

Fig. 4. Notional map of Natun Chamaguri Village.

is inhabited by 245 people, among which 138 (56.33 %) are male and 107 (43.67 %) are female, distributed in 51 households. In Majuli village, the population is neither fixed nor constant as people keep changing their dwelling from one village to another. It is known to all that Majuli is washed out by frequent floods, and villagers have to shift their households from one village to another in search of highland.

Prachin Chamaguri Satra is situated in the Chamaguri cadastral village; the village constitutes of four villages, viz., Mudoi Chuk, Dalani Chamaguri, Kahal Gaon, and Chamaguri Bania Village. The Prachin Chamaguri Satra is situated at a distance of 5 km on the southern side of the Natun Chamaguri Satra. The *satra* was established by Chakrapani Ata, the son of Sankaradeva's daughter Kesavapriya, in the year 1563. Bifurcation is a common feature of a *satra* for various reasons. The Natun Chamaguri Satra was splintered off from the Prachin Chamaguri Satra in the year 1663. The *satra* was established under a very big and old *cham* (*Artocarpus chaplasha*) tree. A few households, who were the devotee of the newly established *satra,* also constructed their houses adjacent to the *satra.* From the historic event of the establishment of the new *satra* under the *cham* tree, the village was known as Natun Chamaguri, which means a new village established under a *cham* tree. The mighty Ahom king Chakradhawja Singha (AD 1663-1670) had helped generously to established the *satra* and also extended help to the devotees and the villagers, and the *satra* flourished under Chakrapani Ata, the founder of the *satra.*

In the *satra,* the *guru* lived with his disciples. A huge prayer hall was constructed at a suitable site. This hall is divided into two parts—*manikut* (literally the store of jewels), and a big open prayer hall. *Manikut* is a room where the scriptures are placed on a staired wooden pedestal known as *asana* (seat), or *guru asana* (seat of the guru). Although a typical *satra* is surrounded by four *hatis,* i.e., the residences of devotees in straight line in all four directions, in the Prachin Chamaguri Satra there are only two *hatis* while in the Natun Chamaguri Satra there is not a single *hati.* It is customary to divide the property of a *satra,* where an offshoot is developed from it, and bifurcate and establish as the new *satra.* It should be noted here that in the Prachin Chamaguri Satra there are a number of hand-written scriptures written and copied by the Vaishnava gurus, some of which are adorned with spectacular multi-coloured drawings. There are also a few wooden and metal objects made and used by the Vaishnava gurus. However, in the Natun Chamaguri Satra, there is not a single hand-written scripture or any object used by the Vaishnava gurus. At the time of bifurcation, the Natun Chamaguri Satra received only two brass metal utensils. Among these, one is a brass *sarai* (disc on stand), and the other one is a *bhogjara,* i.e., a brass pitcher with a spout. At present Sri Koshakanta Deva Goswami, aged 78 years, is the *satradhikar* of the Natun Chamaguri Satra. He is the 14th *satradhikar* from the founder of the Natun Chamaguri Satra. A *satradhikar* is sometimes known as *ata* (grandfather), or *burha satradhikar* (the old abbot). His immediate junior official of the *satra* is known as *deka satradhikar* (pentiff). At present Sri Jadav Goswami, aged 75 years, is the *deka satradhikar* of Natun Chamaguri Satra. Generally, in a *satra* after the death of the *satradhikar,* the *deka satradhikar* succeeds the higher office. However, in the Natun Chamaguri Satra it is the rule to succeed to the post of *satradhikar* after his death by his brother. Traditionally, women were tabooed from entering in a *satra.* But the present *satradhikar* of the Natun Chamaguri Satra has allowed women to pray in the prayer hall in the *satra,* although there is stricture for the women not to enter the *manikut*. The prayer hall of this *satra* has a huge decorative wooden door, and by the side of the door inside there is a big statue of Garuda, the vehicle *(bahana)* of Lord Vishnu. It is believed that Garuda is the keeper of a *satra* who protects the *satra* from all evil. At the rear end of the prayer hall there is a stage for performing the ritualistic theatres called *bhaonas.* The prayer hall is also used to store the mask made by the *satradhikar* and some other persons consanguinally linked to the *satradhikar's* family.

2

Masks in the Context of Culture

Different communities of the world with their varied cultural patterns offer a rich field of research on masks. However, social scientists have not shown any inclination in studying masks from the distant past. Scientific studies on mask are of very recent origin. Initially, masks were studied as integral components of material culture of different societies where masks have conspicuous entity in the social, cultural, and religious life. Apart from its socio-cultural importance and its distribution, systematic studies on it are scanty and rare.

Material cultures of various communities have attracted many scholars and in their studies many of them have included mask as an important trait. Adam (1942) principally dealt with primitive art. He focused on a few masks of East Africa, America, and Oceania, and meticulously described the dance mask of the Bushman, devil mask of the Sinhalese, etc. Underwood (1948) and Trowell (1953) have focused on different masks used by the various tribes of Africa.

Scholars from different disciplines have tried to examine masks from different angles. The stalwart anthropologist Boas (1955) in his noteworthy book *Primitive Art* writes: 'This book is an attempt to give an analytical description of the fundamental traits of primitive art ...'. Here he presents mask as an integral component of the primitive art. He analyzed the art of the primitive people as a sympathetic and sensitive commentator. He systematically delineates the emotional appeal, symbolism, style, medium, etc. and painstakingly examines some of the masks in regard to their integral traits. He describes the wooden mask of Urua of Congo area in the following manner: '...In fig. 65, representing a painted carving from New Guinea, the outline of the face, emphasized by the hair line, eyes, and mouth, is easily recognized, but all the other parts are treated purely decoratively (p. 70)'. Besides, this book contains photographs along with description of some wonderful masks, the names of which are given below:

Tlingit's mask of dying warrior..., carved head of Kwakiutl..., Tlingit's masks representing hawk and symbolizing flicker..., Tlingit's masks symbolizing the squid and killer whale..., and the ornamental mask of Kwakiutl Indians. An idea of Boas' knowledge about mask can be formed by the masterly description of them as exemplified by the following extract about the mask of a dying warrior:

> In a mask... of a dying warrior... representing a dying warrior, the artist has shown faithfully the wide lower jaw, the pentagonal face, and the strong nose of the Indians. The relaxing muscles of mouth and tongue, the drooping eyelids, and the motionless eyeballs, mark the agonies of death. ...... Here belongs also the realistic head previously referred to, made by the Kwakiutl Indians of Vancouver Island (Fig. 156), which is used in a ceremony and intended to deceive the spectators who are made to believe that it is the head of a decapitated dancer (p. 184).

Christensen (1955) deals with masks of different parts of the world: Africa, America, Iroquois, Indonesia, Melanesia, Mexico, Micronesia, Middle America, North-West Pacific Coast, Peru, and South West United States. His book starts with a scholarly introduction about the nature of primitive art, which helps the readers have an idea about the different materials used in mask making, their styles and also their similarities and dissimilarities with other forms of arts found in different parts of the world. While discussing African art, Cordwell (1959) treats mask as an important trait of culture, which forms a conspicuous web adhering to a good number of socio-religious factors. Leuzinger's (1960) *Africa: The Art of Negro People*, translated by Ann E. Keep, discusses the African art including masks of the Negros. The same author, in 1967, thoroughly studied the art of Africa including different types of masks.

Conrad (1967: 253) in his book *The Many Worlds of Man* said: 'Perhaps the best known of all magically related primitive art forms are masks.

These always mysterious, often wild and ferocious looking creations have captured the imagination of civilized men everywhere ..... crucifixes' (p. 253). He observes that Hopi and other Pueblo Indians' spirit mask are more personal. The Hopi hold elaborate ceremonies to please the ancestral spirit several times a year. In such ceremonies they wear painted ancestral mask with integral costumes (p. 188). Fertility mask and healing mask are also indispensable in the Hopi culture. Baluba ceremonial masks made of woven fibre and decorated with shells, bones and feathers reflect the skill, belief, and social cohesion of the society. The Kwakiutl's 'Dramatic mask, which sometimes may be opened to reveal another mask inside, represent spirits, animals and mythological ancestors' (p. 235).

He also examines interrelations of masks in different tribal cultures. In his book there are ten photo plates of picturesque masks with their detailed description. These masks are: Malagan initiation mask (p. 167), Poro mask (p. 172), Bundu mask (p. 173), Hopi and other Pueblo Indians ancestral mask (p. 188), Yoruba fertility mask (p. 208), healing mask of the Iroquois (p. 209), Ibo funeral mask (p. 215), Baluba ceremonial mask (p. 224) made of woven fibre, adorned with shells, bones, and feathers, the mask of renowned wood worker Kwakiutl of Northwest coast representing an eagle (p. 234), and Crested helmet-like mask of New Ireland (p. 251). Malagan is an important rite of New Ireland where the youths are initiated into full manhood and the deceased ancestors are appeased. In this ritual, elaborate masks of stylized boar's head are prepared and used in ritual dance. After use those masks are hung in a special house and allowed to rot. Some of the participants wear crested helmet, like masks depicting clan ancestors. The crest built up with yellow, blue, red, and white fibre over a wooden frame follows the old style of wearing hair during mourning. This mask may also be worn during courtship period. In West Africa, the Gio, Geh, and Mano tribes of Liberia cooperate with Mendi of Sierra Leone and other small neighbouring tribes for mutual benefit. Poro is their inter-tribal secret society, which controls to a large extent the socio-religious life of these tribes. In most of the celebrations, the man integral to the secret society conducts the ritual wearing appropriate masks and costume. Each mask is the abode of a particular spirit, which lends its name to the mask. The masks described in the book are worn in different rituals with the intention of invoking the cooperation of the spirits to increase harvests, to achieve prosperity, etc.

Leiris and Delange (1968) in their book *African Art* discuss the pristine African masks curved in wood and other material. Bondi et al. (1969), while evaluating the arts of the world, have taken mask as one of the important components. They based their study on the objects of art preserved and displayed in Western Museums which were, once according to them, indispensable part of life of many communities. They studied different art objects found in museums as well as in private collections, which do not belong to western culture. They have studied the Indian, Chinese, Japanese, African, Islamic, and the ancient art of Central America. Obviously they have included mask as an integral component of art. The only sixteenth-century ivory mask from Africa included in the book 'representing the *Oba,* or king, of Benin, is topped with a tiara of miniature heads of Portuguese explorers' (p. 44). They have studied art objects in the geo-ethnic context. They write:

> In most cases, however, these art still form part of everyday life. They are picture or objects of use, not simply decoration or a collector's pride or as relief from reality. They are signs and symbols which have powerful social and religious meanings for their creators and their public as our traffic signs have for us. Without some explanation of meaning, of how and why these often complex and strange forms are or were made, we are only getting a fraction of possible enjoyment from them (p.1).

In the Biebuyck's (ed.) book entitled *Traditon and Creativity in Tribal Art* (1969), different authors delineated various aspects of tribal art including the masks of Africa, Pre-Colombian Mexico, etc.

Of these areas, Africa presents two distinct geographical features: the tropical vegetation cover that masks the inner vibrations and rhythm of the people and cultures in it, and Saharan desert, open and wide where the bits of culture sound very feeble. With the advancement of time and under the influence of modernity, the mists surrounding Africa getting thinner and thinner. Of the numerous elements of tribal art, Monte (1969) selected the masks. Some of them disappeared, some are in rare use and others an wane and a few still exist today. The masks to which Monte had an access are mostly from the museums of the West. The most important and significant aspects of his study on masks from the region is that he has made an attempt to relate their cultural values and their meanings within the spectrum of a given ethno-cultural situation characterized by distinctiveness and diversification of the respective groups. The people's voice, mind, and their technical craftsmanship are always space and time specific. The masks very often comvey symbolic meanings to a person though not from within the culture; but to an African who possesses the mask, it creates no communication problem; for him it is neither symbolic, nor abstract; he understands the matter as it is because the mask is a part of the system of which he is a part. Monte's work centres round the narration and detection of morphology, but he did not lose sight of the world view of the inheritors or makers of the masks. He tried to delve into this matter; that he did with limitation.

Duerden has contributed a lot towards the study of mask through his book *African Art* (1970). The book was first published in 1968, and its first paperback edition came out in 1970. In this book Duerden has examined the different objects of art found among various tribal groups of Africa like carved door, cave painting, door post, fabric, figure, mask, plaque, throne, walls of house with mud decoration, etc. The book possesses an ethnographic map and Duerden tries to relate each object of art to the socio-religious matrix of integral societies. The book is adorned with nineteen plates of mask with their description, which highlight the physical characteristics of the masks along with their social, cultural, religious, and geographical significance. The following are the masks mentioned in the book:

Helmet mask of the Do Gurdian Spirit of the Bobo Fing people living in the Bobo Djulasso area, Upper Volta; Kurumba dancer's mask; Nmwo society mask of the Ibo, Eastern Nigeria; mask of the Ekpo society of the Ibibio, Eastern Nigeria; Beteke mask of Congo; Shene Malula mask of central Congo; Kalebue mask of Congo-Kinshasa; Toma mask of Guinea; Atye mask of Ivory Coast; Bambara mask of Mali; Bafo mask of Cameroons; Bakwele mask of Congo-Brazzaville; Bacham mask of Cameroon; Bapende mask of Congo-Kinshasa; Dogon mask of Upper Volta; Yoruba mask of Dahomey; Baule mask of Ivory Coast; Mark mask of French Sudan; and Bayaka mask of Congo-Kinshasa. There are two plates of Bami Elke masqueraders (plates 19 and 20), which are adorned with elaborate costumes including head-dresses which are artistic expansion of masks. Most of the masks are made of wood and are sometimes adorned with fibre, grass, shells, etc. The height of the masks varies from 9 inches to 35½ inches.

Sannes (1970) meticulously describes forty masks and figures of West Africa. Wassing's (1970) painstaking study on African art is another important work on the study of masks where he explores the mask of the different tribes of Africa. Laude's (1971) book, *The Arts of Black Africa,* translated by Jean Decock, has made immense contribution towards the study of arts including that of mask. The book contains eight chapters and Laude devotes chapter V (137-180) to the systematic description of the internal feature of masks of Africa. He traces the history of African mask, its relation to ritual and ceremony, and its link with spirituality. He has divided the African masks into the following types, viz., leaf and woven mask, facial mask, helmet mask, blade-shaped mask, and mask crowned by sculptures. Most of the masks are made of wood, sometimes painted or with fibre added to it. A sixteenth-century mask of Benine, Nigeria (p. 159) is made of ivory. Almost all the masks are worn vertically; however, there are some masks which are worn horizontally. In the Translator's Preface of the book, the translator Decock has rightly pointed out:

> 'Laude's work is valuable, far from ignoring the ambiguities of a particular approach, the paralyzing absence of criteria, and the limitations of the data, he takes them all into account and integrate them into a synthesis which is thereby the best possible introduction to African arts. His triple pre-occupation is to describe the diversified expression of creative artists, to define their specificity by relating it to societies and cultural environment, and to evaluate the personal techniques of the artists. Laude's work grows towards a totalization, because it relates metaphysical implications, spatial dimension, and historical perspective (p. vii).

Maquet, through his book *Africanity: The Cultural Unity of a Black Africa,* published in 1972, translated by Field, has assessed the unique cultural heritage shared by many people of black Africa. Professor Maquet shows how analogous existential experiences of life in an isolated and difficult environment have slowly produced a unified African world distinct from, and comparable to, the Western and Asian worlds. This unity, he asserts, is not racial but cultural; and it does not encompass blacks living outside of sub-Saharan Africa. The book altogether contains five articles on different aspects of African culture, which are: A Cultural Continent, The Sources of Africanity, The Contents of Africanity, Prospect for Africanity, and One Hundred Traditional Societies. In the last article of the book *One Hundred Traditional Societies,* the author has provided meticulous description of hundred African societies, drawn up and prepared by Jean-Claude Schalchli. He describes their socio-religious and economic life along with their craftsmanship. The author has also made an attempt to throw light on the different varieties of masks used by these indigenous tribes, and the materials used by them to prepare those, and their use and utility.

Delange (1974) has broadened our knowledge by delineating the masks of different communities of Africa where one can have a transparent picture of Bayiri mask, Chiwara mask, Fulse-Mossi mask, Kore lion mask, Ndomo mask, and Sirige mask. William's (1974) notable book *Icon and Image: A Study of Sacred and Secular Form of African Classical Art* has examined the history, material culture, mask, oral tradition, and sculptures of Africa.

Gillison writes two papers; in one (1977) he deals with the ways of life, including rituals of a village of New Guinea where he refers to a Bark mask. In the other paper (1983) he delineates the Gimi-speaking Eastern Highlanders of Papua New Guinea. In the Gimi folk performances locally made masks are indispensable. Gillon describes the gourd mask and flat mask of the eastern highlanders. In his book *Collecting African Art* (1979), he offers careful study of African arts including masks. McDowell, in his book *The Aztecs* (1980: 704-752), makes valuable contribution to the study of mask. While studying the Aztec culture and history, he examines the importance of various leather masks and Tlaloc masks used in that culture. Macdonald's (1981: 52-56) paper entitled *Masks in Kalimantan Timur* deals with the masks of Kalimantan, which are known as *hadoq* or *udog*. Most of their masks have animal forms, though other forms of masks are also found in Kalimantan.

Emigh (1981) explores the mask of New Guinea used in different ceremonies. He writes about the Tubun mask, and the making of Kavat mask by the Bainings people. In the paper *Masked Dances of the Yoruba People,* Ojo (1981: 37- 48) deals briefly with the masks of the Yorubas used in different ceremonies. Levi-Strauss's (1983) book *La Voie des Masques,* translated by Sylvia Modelelski as *The Way of the Masks,* 'can be considered as an introduction to structuralism, based on the concepts of opposition and dialectical meaning'. According to Levi-Strauss, masks should not be treated as separate objects, but as objects associated with myths of the communities. Napier (1986) focuses masks in relation to 'crisis' rites and 'curative' ceremonies. He opines that the special efficacy of a mask lies in transforming a person, because it invariably suppresses the identity of the wearer, and projects him as a different person. Fenton (1987) assesses the Iroquois mask where he refers to twelve types of masks like the crooked-mouth mask, hanging mouth mask, smiling mask, spoon-lipped mask or spoon-mouthed mask, etc. Ions (1987) explains man's behaviour, agony, superstitions, etc. including a few masks of the tribes of North-West coast. He meticulously describes some of the masks like Aztec, Bapende (Congo), Iroquois, Mende (Sierra Leone), Mossi (Upper Volta), Mpongwe (Congo), Poro, Senufo (Ivory Coast), Yoruba, etc. Bancroft-Hunt (1988) describes the Kwakiutl mask, Tlingit hawk spirit mask, Tsimshian sun and wooden seal mask. These masks are integral to the ceremonial dances of the said tribe.

Eyo (1990), writing on the art of Nigeria, offers thought-provoking descriptions of the Bass-Nge mask, Edo village (Ekpo) mask, Egungun masks, Epa masks, Gelede masks, Ibibio (Ekpo) masks, Mama (Mangam) cap masks, Mambila mask, Ogoni masks, and Ogun mask. In the book *Nok Terracottas*, Fagg (1990) explores the varieties of Nok art. In this context, he describes the mask of the Epas, Ibibias, and Oduduwas. Mark (1992), in his book *The Wild Bull and the Sacred Forest: Form, Meaning, and Change in Senegambian Initiation Masks*, discusses the masks of the Jola society. He explores the ritual symbolism of those masks and elaborately describing the horned initiation masks, and traditional masks of the Jolas. Heppell (1992), in his book *Masks of Kalimantan*, assesses the masks of a number of relatively isolated communities inhabiting the Kalimantan islands. He describes the Dayak religion of the inhabitants where masks are an indispensable part. He explores what the various masks represent, and why they are used in some particular situations. He has meticulously described the Berawan mask, Dayak mask, Kayan mask, Mahakam mask, Melanau mask, Ngaju mask, Sampit mask, etc.

Nooter (1993) deals particularly with the late nineteenth and twentieth century of sub-Saharan African culture where she finds that some masks are used for the sake of secrecy. Kerchache et al. in their book *Art of Africa* (1993) delineate a few masks of the different communities of Africa as an integral part of their study. Lechuga and Sayer's (1994) *Mask Art of Mexico* is another important addition to the study of mask. It explores in detail the Mexican masks, majority of which show human faces with male features. Carnival, Holy Week, Feast days devoted to local patron saint known as Las Fiestas Patronales, the Days of the dead, etc. are some of the important ceremonial occasions in Mexico where the masks are worn. Mack (1994), in his edited book entitled *Masks: The Art of Expression*, has provided indispensable understanding of masks. He narrates convincingly the mask's features and examines the relation of masks with masquerade, and speaks about the circumstances of their use. The notable study of Wyatt (1994) contributed immensely towards the study of mask. He focuses on the spirit masks of North-West Coast, which are an integral part of the ceremonial life of the tribes of the region. In their dance dramas they invariably use the mask of the demons and deities through which one can have a picture of their cultural life. He has meticulously described the Clan mask, Crest mask, Narrative mask, Shaman mask, and Transformation mask of North-West Coast.

McCune (1962) explores the masks of Korea, especially the good luck mask, the mask for exorcizing pimple spirit, monk mask, and monkey mask, worn during carnival, painted wooden mask, shaman mask, etc. Coomaraswamy (1965) assesses the masks used by the players in dance dramas in Combodia, Java, Khon mask play, and Wayang Topeng mask play. Bowra (1966) examines Greek theatres where masks are indispensable. Those theatres are performed in a vast stage in front of a huge gathering, where communication is very difficult between the actors and the spectators. To overcome the situation, the actors wear terracotta masks of man, woman, young, old, happy, or melancholic person. Woldering in his book *Gods, Men and Pharaohs: The Glory of Egyptian Art* (1967: 151-52) principally focuses on the Egyptian art, where he elaborately describes a mask worn by the male from Amarana. Osborne (1968) outlines the mythology and culture of America and correlates different masks of the region. He particularly deals with the red ceramic stylized mask of the Chibcha Indians of Guatavita of Colombia, and the mummy mask of the Mochica culture. Ambesi's (1970) book *Oceanic Art* is actually the translated version of the Italian book *Arte dell' Oceania*, which was published in 1966. Rachel Montgomery has translated the book. Ambesi writes:

> Oceanic art does not aim at an ideal of beauty, or the expression of some emotional need, but attempts to bridge two very different worlds—on the one hand the world of the collective unconscious prefer

> natural powers, and on the other the world of myths, legends and influences rooted in the world of the gods. Its function is thus quite different from that of most western art: a fact which is essential to bear in mind at every point in this book (p.7).

Masks are an integral part of the Oceanic beliefs and, therefore, among different communities of Oceania, the use of mask in different rites and situation is a common feature. The book is filled with the details of the art objects, with their spiritual and religious significance.

Locke and Savill (1976: 180-186) write about the Gold death mask, known as 'mask of Agamemnon' in their article *Classical Greece and Rome, Narrative Outlines: Greece Legends of the House of Pelops.* Paine in his book *The Art and Architecture of Japan* (1974) presents a detailed study of the art and architecture of the country and projects mask to that as an important object of Japanese art. Adams (1979) explores the masks of Korea, which are the integral objects of their dance drama, and also an indispensable trait of Korean folk traditions. Aubert (1980) explores the mask of Switzerland majority of which are folkloric mask. Behague (1980) discusses the cultures of South America where ceremonial and ritual dances play pivotal role in the socio-religious matrix of society. The performers of many such dances used to wear different types of masks, especially the tribal communities such as the Chuncho of Peru, the Vitoto, Uanana, and Tariana of Columbia, the Tukuna tribe of Upper Amazon region, and the different tribes of the upper Xingu of Brazil. Bonnefoy (1981: Vol.I) focuses on the ivory mask and wooden (teak) mask, etc. of Africa. In Vol. II (1981) he studies the Chinese and New Caledonia masks. In the *Da-nuo* dance, the actor used to wear a mask with four eyes to represent the deity Fangxiang. Bonnefoy describes the New Caledonia mask, which represents the guardian of the dead land. A noteworthy contribution on mask is made by Iteanu (1981). The study was based on the people in islands from the east of Indonesia to Easter Island. These islands are divided into three distinct traditional divisions—Melanesia, Polynesia, and Micronesia. The uses of mask in Polynesia and Micronesia are rare. In Polynesia, a few specially stylized masks are used in mourning ceremonies. In Lukunor, Morlock, and Satawan Islands of Micronesia, masks are used to decorate the dwelling houses. But in Melanesian societies, plenty of masks are found, which play dominating role in the art, culture, and rituals of the inhabitants.

Piggott (1982) outlined the mask used in the Noh plays of the Japanese where the performers used different types of masks. Nicholsen (1983) explores the complex culture of Maya, Nahua, and Central America, where he shows a few masks as integral components of their culture. In the book *Indonesian Primitive Art*, Hersey (1991) delineates different masks like Batak mask, Batak topeng mask, Flores mask, Iban devil mask, and Timor face mask. *The Arts of Japan* (1991, two volumes), translated by Rasenfield, explores the Japanese art and craft. The book also gives a brief description of the masks of Japan. Baker (1992) discusses the Noh masks of Japan. In the book *Classical Dance and Theatre in South-East Asia*, Miettinen (1992) mainly explores the heritage of classical tradition of South-East Asian dance, mask theatre, and puppet theatre, where he shows masks as integral components of performing arts. While describing the tribal arts of North America, Feest (1994) mentions a few masks of the area.

In Java, a mask is known as *topeng*, which is most widely used the region. Fischer (1994) explores the folk art of Java where he focuses on the dance dramas and the masks used in these dramas. Sharer (1994) explores the Mask of ancient Maya, particularly the Zade mask, God mask, and Mosaic mask. Warren and Tettoni (1994) focus on Thai theatre and show the mask as integral objects of the theatre. Ben-Amos (1995) in his book *The Art of Benin* explores the mask used in dance and other rituals of Benin (West Africa). Vital information on performing arts of Asia, especially that of Bali, is discussed by Emigh (1996). He made a thorough study on the making of the masks of the region with comments on their various designs. According to Emigh, these masks exhibit imaginative power of the inhabitants of the region. Chandavij and Pramualratna in their book entitled *Thai Puppets and Khon Mask* (1998) deal with the masks worn by the dancers in performing art. The dance dramas based on *The Ramayana* are very popular there, and the dancers wear ornately fashioned gilded masks. Barbier (2000) studies five Pre-Columbian masks in the style of Teotihuacan, and stone masks from Teotihuacan.

Pani (1986), in his book *World of Other Faces: Indian Mask*, explores different aspects of masks principally in four chapters of the book, viz., Mask and Ritual, Mask and Theatre, The Pliant Masks, and Mask and Contemporary Theatre. The study area of Pani is India, and he has cited numerous examples of masks from every nook and corner of the country.

However, he has totally ignored Assam, although the state has a rich heritage of mask. Dey and Irwin (1947) in their book *The Folk Art of Bengal* evaluated mainly the folk art of Bengal including the earthen masks. Dhaninivat and Yupho (1954) assessed the Khon dance where the performers use mask. It should be noted here that Khon is one of the Thai classical dances where mask plays a vital role. These masks have a wide variety of designs to indicate the role or character of the wearers. Uppal (1959: 26-30) discusses three distinct streams of folk dance in Bihar, and focuses masks as indispensable components of Chhau dance. Devi (1966: 46-48) elaborates the festivals performed to appease goddess Bhagabati of Kerala, and outlines the integral ritualistic form of masked dance performed at the temples of goddess Kali in Travancore during mid-March to mid-June. The masked dance is known as Kolamthullal. Dhamija (1966) in his article 'Masks' in *Marg* contributed considerably towards the study of Chhau mask of Seraikella and the masks of Chotanagpur area. Anand (1968) elaborately describes the mask used by Chhau dancers.

Kothari (1968: 5-24) wrote an article on Chhau dance of Saraikella on its origin, its ritualistic techniques and points out that mask was an integral part of the said dance. He (1979: 81-91) also wrote a paper on the sacred dance drama of Kerela known as Kathakali where the performers painted their faces and wore partial masks. In the article *The Use of Masks in Indian Dances and Dance Dramas*, Kothari (1980: 89-103) opines that from the initial stage of Indian performing arts, masks were used. He also wrote that the origin of masks in India can be traced back to the rites and rituals and folk ceremonies. The Lama ritual dances of Arunachal Pradesh and Ladakh support this view. Till today, in some of the tribal and folk performing arts, masks are invariably used. In some of the living dance drama tradition of India like *Ankiya nat* of Assam, Bhagavata Mela Nataka of Melattur in Tanjore district of Tamil Nadu, Chhau dances of Bihar and West Bengal, Krishnatta of Kerala, Kusipudi dance drama of Andhra Pradesh, Ramalila of Benaras, Rasalila of Manipur, and Sahi Jatra of Orissa, masks are worn by the dancers. In Chhau dances of Bihar and West Bengal, all the dancers invariably wear masks. Pani (1968: 32-45) outlines the origin and evolution of Chhau dance of Mayurbhanj. In 1969 (35-45), the same author presents a comparative study of the Chhau dances performed in Mayurbhanj and Sareikela.

Elwin (1969) describes a few masks and their role in the social, cultural, and religious matrix of various societies of North-East India in the book *The Art of North-East India. A Philosophy for NEFA* (1964) is a noteworthy book on the geo-ethnic situation of Arunachal Pradesh, then NEFA, in which Elwin has depicted the life way of the different communities of that region along with various problems of the people. Many communities of the region have the tradition of mask making. It is interesting to note that while discussing health problems of the people, Elwin had to mention a 'Monpa mask representing a woman with exophthalmic goiter' (p.89). He writes:

> Along the northern frontier, the Monpas and Sherdukpens, the Membas and Khambas have a large repertory of ceremonial pantomimes, which the mummers perform in gorgeous dresses and finely carved and painted masks, during the chief festivals of the Buddhist year (p. 266).

In the book entitled *The Tribals of Middle India: A Personal Record,* Elwin (1951: 136-150) devotes a chapter to masks. His study area covers Madhya Pradesh, and parts of Bihar, and Orissa. In that chapter he has included 15 photo plates of masks used by the Baiga, Bhuiya, Gond, Kond, Kuttia, and the Muria tribes. Most of the masks are made from wood and bottle gourd shell, decorated with bell-metal piece, gourd seeds, bear's hair, etc. Some of the masks are painted meticulously. These masks are principally used for ceremonial and recreational dances. Elwin writes: "It is not easy to discover mask in tribal India, for they are normally only brought out on ceremonial occasions and for some reason the aboriginals are rather shy about them and not very willing to show them to the inquirer" (p.136). *Regional Dances: Orissa - Dormitory Performance of the Murias* of Elwin (1959) focuses on the gourd mask, and the masked dance of the Murias. Elwin (1969) also describes a few masks and their role in the social, cultural and religious matrix of various societies of North-East India.

Khoker writes two articles on masks. In the article *Regional Dances: Kerala* (1959), he explores dance as an integral part of the life of the inhabitants of Kerala. The people of Kerala inextricably related to dance. In some of the dances, masks are used which are surmounted on the bases of latticed coconut leaves and gorgeously painted according to the features of a character. In the year 1989, he wrote another article on centuries-old Thiyan tradition wherein different festival masks are used. It should be noted here that these masks are used only once and then these are thrown away. In the year 1986, Khoker in his book on tradition of Indian classical dance explores Chhau dance performed in three different states, namely, Mayurbhanj Chhau, Purulia Chhau, and Seraikella Chhau. He opines that Mayurbhanj and Seraikella versions of Chhau seem to have originated from the same root. However, in Mayurbhanj, Chhau masks are not used while in Serraikella all Chhau dances are performed with masks. In the Purulia form of Chhau dances also, masks are used. He (1981) points out that the dance of Seraikella in Bihar and Mayurbhanj in Orissa, are two distinct and different traditions of Chhau dance. However, in both the places these dances are performed only once in a year during Chitra Parva, a ritual performed in March-April using gorgeous costumes.

Singh's (1970) book entitled *Himalayan Art* is the first of a new series of the UNESCO Art Books where he treats the geographical area of the Himalayas, particularly Ladakh, Lahual and Spiti, the Siwalik Ranges, Nepal, Sikkim, and Bhutan, where varieties of cultural waves synthesized and persisted to the present time. This book principally interprets the little known but significant traits of material culture in relation to the social culture. In this book, Singh observes that masks are an integral part of the different cultures of the Himalayan region. The book also contains some attractive photographs of masks with relevant descriptions. He describes the 'wooden mask', for example, in the following manner:

> A wooden mask (p. 103) is a fantastic piece of workmanship, simple yet effective. It is a reflection of the spirits and devils of Bon-po beliefs about magic, sorcery, and superstition. On gay festive occasions and at times of ill-fortune, these replicas of mountain images are worn by traditional dancers, who invariably appear on the scene to assist the occasion with their slow rhythm, in tune to deep-sounding drums echoing in the valleys. The Bon-po cult has been suspended by the Buddhist religion, but these basic art forms of an ageless variety are firmly enshrined in the mental make-up and religious and artistic responses of the hardy, truthful, and kind hearted people of Lahaul and Spiti.

Besides the wooden mask, the book describes two marvelous masks of Devi (p. 137) made of copper and silver. Both the masks are representative traits of the Siwalik Range culture. Singh (1971) describes three masks of the Himalayan region, viz., the copper and silver masks of goddess Bhakti, and a wooden mask from Lahaul Valley.

Bhattacharyya (1972) deals with the Chhau dance, the mask used in that dance, and also about the Chhau mask makers of Purulia, West Bengal. In the book *Chhau: Mask Dance of Saraikela,* Deo (1973) examines in detail the mask used in the Chhau dance. Bhavnani (1974) describes folk and tribal designs of India including the dance and drama, where masks of malevolent and benevolent spirits, human beings, and comic characters are part and parcel. In Orissa, wooden masks are used by different artists to depict the stories of the *Ramayana* and the *Mahabharata. Paper Mache* masks generally represent Durga, the goddess of strength and power. All the masks highlight the nature and personalities of the characters represented by the actors. Chattopadhyay (1976) in her book *The Glory of Indian Handicrafts* deals with some of the masks in the section entitled 'Theatre Crafts'. She discusses a good number of dances and the masks used in them in this section. In the book *Handicrafts of India* (1985), Chattopadhyay elaborately discusses the process and techniques of handicrafts of India. In the 'Theatre Craft' section of the book, she provides thought-provoking information about some masks from different parts of India. Pannikar (1979: 107-110) discusses five forms of folk dances of Kerala where he focuses masks as integral to the dances. Furer-Haimendorf's (1972) *The Sherpas of Nepal: Buddhist Highlanders* is the first anthropological study of the Sherpas, who dwell in the valleys at the foot of the Mount Everest Massif. Despite a non-congenial climate and extreme altitude of their habitat, the polyandrous Sherpas have developed a pattern of life which is rich in social, aesthetic, and spiritual accomplishments. Long back, they had professed Buddhism; yet, some of the traits of their pristine animistic faith are still present in the Sherpa society. The monasteries play a vital role in the life of the Sherpas where there are a good number of annual and occasional rites, some of which are elaborately observed with pomp and gaiety. As for example, Mani Rimdu, a ritual of monastery feast and ritual dances, is performed for four consecutive days. Dances are an integral part of the prayer and other ritual activities of Mani Rimdu. In some of the dances of this ritual, masks are used by the dancers with appropriate costumes. Furer- Haimendorf has elaborately described the ritual, dances, and the masks used therein and discussed their significance.

Brauen (1980) deals with the festivals of Ladakh, particularly the mask dance festival. The book contains some eye-catching illustrations of mask dances. Vatsyayan (1980) explains the multiple streams of traditional Indian theatre where she describes the mask of Chhau dance practised in Bihar, Orissa, and West Bengal. In the year 1987 the same author outlined folk dances of India, particularly the mask dance of Ladakh and Chhau dance, where masks are an integral part of Mayurbhanj, Purulia, and Seraikella. Banerji (1982) in his book *Aesthetics of Indian Folk Dance* describes different masks used in traditional dances of India. According to Banerji, in Indian folk dances masks have a marked significance. He describes the mask of Orissa worn in *Ramalila* (broadly, the life of Lord Vishnu's incarnation as Rama), and that of the devil dance masks of the hill tribes. He also describes the Thera Yattam mask of South India, and records the materials used and the process of making it. Ambrose (1983) in his book *Classical Dances and Costumes of India* describes elaborately Chhau dance, an ancient form of ritualistic folk expression performed at Seraikella and Mayurbhanj of West Bengal. Chhau dance is performed only by the males, who even play the female roles. Use of mask is indispensable in Chhau dance, and the dancers wear both male and female masks. Grund (1985), explores the Chhau dance of Mayurbhanj, Purulia, and Seraikella, where he describes mask as an integral part of the dance. In the same year (1985) he studied Chhau dances of Bihar, Orissa, and West Bengal. Grund opines that the origin, techniques, and integral ritual of Chhau dance vary in these three regions. Chhau dances are invariably performed by males using masks, particularly the one performed during the harvesting period. Saraf (1985) outlined the origin of Indian craft of mask making, its development and potentiality, and traced the link between various painted wooden masks of Surya, the Sun god of Bihar, Karnataka, and the mask of Moon god, and Ravana, the mighty demon-king, used in Orissa.

Keay (1986) studied in detail the history and culture of the people of Ladakh and explored a few Tiksey masks. The stalwart anthropologist Vidyarthi (1993) mentions some aspects of masks of North-East India while describing the art and culture of this remote part of India. Massey and Massey (1989) discuss the masks integral to Chhau dance of Mayurbhanj, Purulia, and Seraikella. The focal point of Amatya's (1991) book *Art and Culture of Nepal* is the Nepalese art. In the book, the author writes a chapter on the masks of Nepal, which are used in some of their dances and the dramas. These masks are made only in the Kathmandu Valley, and in Solu Khumbu area in the northern part of

Nepal. Aryan (1991) principally describes the bronze masks from various parts of India including the *Devi* (goddess) mask of Karnataka, and traditional masks of Kullu. Burfank (1991) in his book *Nepal* describes the culture, economy, life ways, religion, etc. of Nepal including the traditional dramas which are principally based on the *Ramayana* and the *Mahabharata,* and performed during the religious festivals to propitiate the gods and goddesses. The performers wear various masks representing different gods and goddesses. In the book *The Masks of God: Primitive Mythology,* Campbell (1991) has examined the bases of the mythology of the world, and also discusses the ceremonial masks. He has examined the mythology of the world from the points of view of anthropology and on the basis of recent discoveries of archaeology and psychology.

Gargi's (1991) book *Folk Theatre of India* focuses on the varieties of pristine performing arts of India and describes in detail the mask worn by the dancers in the Chhau dance. Konishi (1997: 43-55) in his paper 'Masks and Performing Arts: India and Japan', tells us about the influence of Indian mask on the mask of Japan. He describes the influences of the Asura mask of Orissa on the Koygen mask of rural Japan, Charkhilaini mask of West Bengal on Ama mask of Bugaku, Garuda mask of Assam on Karura mask worn in Gigaku dance, the Gond-ritual mask of Baster, Madhya Pradesh, on the Dengaku mask, Raksasi and Siknidhal masks worn in Gambhira dance of West Bengal on Satokaguru mask on Gyodo or Ki-raigo mask worn by the artists in Japan, respectively. Pal (1991) presents the art of Nepal and Tibet and discusses the mask-like sculptures of Nepali culture. Aryan (1993) delineates various folk arts of Himachal Pradesh and describes a few masks. Rajakaruna (1993: 17-22) in his paper 'The Classical Noh Theatre of Japan: An Indian Approach' examines whether the concept of *abhinaya* (acting) elaborated in the *Natyasastra* is applicable to the oldest classical theatre of Japan, known as Noh theatre. Some of the performers in Noh used to wear different types of mask.

Venu (1993: 10-16) prepares a report on mask dances organized by Natana Kairali of Kerala, from 24th October to 1st November, 1992. Natana Kairali is a research and performing centre for folk arts and organized some workshops where elaborate discussions were made on the functions, rituals, and underlying concepts of masks. In the book *Crafts of West Bengal,* Sen (1994) provides a conspicuous scenario of the cultural heritage of West Bengal. He delineates a good number of forms of crafts practised in different parts of Bengal, and focuses on the Chhau mask of the state. 'The Chhau Dance of Mayurbhanj', the paper written by Patnaik (1997: 19-30; 1998: 127-128; 1999: 21-43), covers the Chhau dance of Bihar, Orissa, and West Bengal. He discusses in detail the origin, history, and technical aspects of Chhau dance in the said regions. During the Chaitra Parva, a ceremony performed in March-April, various dances were held where the performers used different masks of the Hindu mythological characters. Chatterjee (1998) discusses 400 masks from 21 countries exhibited in an international mask festival organized in New Delhi jointly by the Indira Gandhi National Centre for the Arts, Indian Council of Cultural Relations, National School of Drama, and Sangeet Nataka Academy. Pate (1998: 85-95) discusses the devil dance mask of Sri Lanka, which is a fast-fading culture. Traditionally, this dance was integral to the socio-cultural matrix of the inhabitants of Sri Lanka. He tells that in Natima devil dances, masks are invariably used. Mask dance ceremonies are performed by the people of Sri Lanka to get rid of death and crop failure, drought, hindrances in pregnancy, etc.

Vergati (1999) explores the masks of deities and demons of Kathmandu Valley of Nepal, where she explains the relation between the dancers and the masks. The valley is inhabited mainly by the Newars and in their society after wearing a particular mask, the wearer is accepted as a god or a demon by the fellow members. In the desk diary *The Mask Tradition of India* (2000), ceremonial, festive, and decorative masks of India have been discussed. In the *Rupa-Pratirupa: Mind Man and Mask,* edited by Malik (2001), there are 35 intense, complex, stimulating papers on masks of different communities of the world. Probably, it is the only book from India which delineates masks vividly from the prehistoric period to the present time. In the different papers of the book, the mask is viewed and analyzed from different angles.

It is unfortunate that although the entire North-East India has a great heritage of making and using masks in different contexts, yet significant writings on mask of this remote part of India are very scanty. The scholarly study of Pani (1986) is a notable work, which includes a good number of masks integral to rituals and performing arts of different communities of India, but also sadly ignores the age-old tradition of masks in North-East India. Malik's (ed.) book on different aspects of masks includes only one article written by Mahanta (2001: 171-75) where the writer makes only some sporadic remarks on masks of Assam mainly related to different performing arts of Assam. However, in the article 'Majulir Mukha Silpar Parampara aru Carcha' (the tradition and practice of mask at Majuli) written in Assamese, Goswami (2001: 141-43), a mask maker of repute, depicts the tradition and traits of the Vaishnavite masks of Majuli.

Neog (1959: 9-20) explores the folk dances of Assam (undivided) in some of which masks play an indispensable role. A few tribes of NEFA (now Arunachal Pradesh) wear wooden masks in folk dances. He has also described the masks used by the *dhulias* (the drummers), a performing art of Lower Assam. Roy (1984-85: 57-60) elaborates different dimensions of masks, particularly from Arunachal Pradesh and the plains of Assam, preserved in the museum of the department of Anthropology, Gauhati University. These masks are mainly carved out from wood and some are made of paper pulp, and basketry and textile with a coat of clay over it. The masks are primarily associated with magico-religious beliefs, but differ owing to the socio-economic and ecological conditions. These masks are not only the symbols of fear, war, and death, but also are symbolic characters of legends.

Medhi is the lone scholar who has continuously worked on the Vaishnavite masks of Assam. In the year 2003, Medhi wrote a few articles in local news-papers and magazines, which are directly or indirectly related to the masks of Majuli. In the article *Ajan Udar Satradhikarar Sannidhyat* (literally 'in the association of a magnanimous head of a Vaishnavite monastery'; 2003, a: 4), he writes about Sri Koshakanta Deva Goswami, principal abbot of the Natun Chamaguri Satra, who is a receipent of Sangeet Nataka Academy award for his noteworthy skill of mask making. Medhi (2003, b: 7) writes in *Matrika Majuli* (literally 'the divine mother of Majuli') about the salient geo-ethnic features of Majuli along with its archaic mask-making culture. *Majulir Mukha* (literally 'Masks of Majuli'; 2003 c: 4) is another thought-provoking article where he discussed in detail about the mask-making tradition of Majuli. In the essay *Parangat Mukha Khanikar Hem Chandra Goswami* (literally 'expert mask maker Hemchandra Goswami'; 2003, d: 35), Medhi delineates about a stalwart mask maker, viz., Hemchandra Goswami of Natun Chamaguri Satra of Majuli. This article is accompanied by six pictures of the colourful masks made by this famous mask-maker. In two articles, *Majulir Maydanava* (literally 'the expert mask maker of Majuli like the demon Moy'; 2003, e: 2), and *Pratibandheer Parakashtha* (literally 'extreme skill of a physically challenged person'; 2003, f: 2) Medhi describes the marvellous mask making skill of a physically challenged person, viz., Sri Dharmakanta Goswami of Natun Chamaguri Satra, Majuli. 'Behind the Mask' (29th August, 2003; g) is another article of Medhi on mask making process, status of mask makers, use of masks, etc. in Majuli island. In the year 2006 (585-586), the same author wrote an article entitled 'Mukha' (masks) in *Viswakosh,* the encyclopedia in Assamese, where he focuses on the salient feature of masks of the *satras* of Assam. Medhi's *Mukha Sambandhe Jatkinchit* (literally 'modicum of masks'; 2007: 49-50) is about the mask-making process and its integral traits as prevalent in Majuli.

Medhi and Zaman (2004: 4-8) describe the mask makers of the Vaishnavite monasteries of Majuli, in which the role and status of the mask makers, their socialization process related to mask making, and the uses of masks have been discussed. In the paper 'Tradition of Mask at a Vaishnavite Monastery in Majuli of Assam', Medhi and Zaman (2008: 213-24) describe meticulously the important features integral to the masks of the Chamaguri Satra of the river island Majuli, Assam.

Though the above review is not exhaustive by any means, yet it indicates the general nature of the study on masks and the aspects which are focused on.

3

Prologue to Mask

3.1 UNDERLYING MEANING OF MASK

The mask is commonly understood to conceal the real identity of a person; but often by wearing mask, a person unmasks his unexpressed aspirations and desired for a time being. Masks are actually artificial faces worn as disguise usually to frighten or to assume. It is also used to protect and hide the face and to conceal feelings. It is pertinent to note that the word 'person' is derived from a Greek word 'persona', which means 'mask', more accurately 'the role played by an actor in a dramatic performance'. Mask has the ability to hide a person's identity and to reveal him as another being. The capacity of hiding and revealing is integral to each mask. Generally, a mask is worn over the face. However, painting over the face integral to rituals and festivals, in a number of societies, is also treated as a mask. This type of mask remains only for a limited period and is erased after the ritual. According to Laude (1971: 142):

> The widely diverse appearance taken by masks shows clearly that they must absorb the totality of the energy spread throughout the world. Indeed masks differ from statuary in that they often combine human and animal characteristics, producing composite monsters with traits of several species. They present the most varied theme and contain many fantastic and imaginary elements.

A mask assumes diverse forms. The principal motive in creating a mask is probably, magico-religious need, which is connected with the mundane activities of everyday life. Though the oldest evidence of masks are found in the cave walls and rock shelters of Upper Palaeolithic Period in the form of arts created by our hunter ancestors, the tradition did not end even after man entered into the higher form of culture. The early ancestors' limitation to control nature, and uncertainty and obstacles of life were also present in the so-called advanced societies. Therefore, like the 'primitives', the people of advanced societies also resort to mask, through which they believed hindrances of life could be overcome. Overwhelming majority of the masks represents malevolent spirits; however, both malevolent and benevolent masks are made and used as a means to achieve peace, pleasure, and prosperity, and finally ensuring the cultural existence overcoming the hazards of life.

> The term mask may be defined in many ways and contextualized in as many also. From prehistoric times (as seen in rock art) masks have been an integral part of pre- and non-industrial societies in the ritual context in order to reveal the many dimensions of existential reality. For example, appeasement of the elements, celebrations of seasons, pleasing the gods, promoting fertility, fighting the demons and enemies, wearing animal masks in order to gain power attributed to those animals; and other masks that help to unravel the mysteries of the unknown by being in touch with the enigmatic mythic-divinity through transforming one's social identity by assuming the archetypal prototype roles. From a religious function of the mask, to the related carnival one, there is a continuum as the wearer is allowed to transport him/herself to distant realms of fantasy, obviously expressed differently in the varied traditional socio-cultural contexts (Malik, 2001: 50).

From time immemorial, masks are related to the primordial thought process indispensably related to innumerable cultures, and beliefs about masks abound in every community. Masks also have a deep significance in the socio-cultural study of a community with a custom of mask making.

> The human body is like a mask. Life wears it as it acts. When Death pulls down the final curtain, life stops acting and discards the mask. Then it is revealed.
>
> The face which gives the body its identity is also its quintessence. If the face is masked it becomes another face. The body too becomes another body because it feels that a new being flows in from the mask. That

> 'being' seizes upon the body and transforms it so that there is no inconsistency between the new face and the new body. Thus masks act as an instrument of metamorphosis, especially when the mind is as impressionable as that of a primitive man (Pani, 1986: 1).

Art is not an isolated phenomenon. It is part of a culture linked up with the history of that culture and the history of the people. Mask is a form of art and it has a thought-provoking history of evolution. Boas (1955: 10) writes:

> What then gives to the sensation and aesthetic value? When the technical treatment has attained a certain standard of excellence, when the control of the process involved is such that certain typical forms are produced, we call the process an art, and however simple the forms may be, they may be judged from the point of formal perfection; industrial pursuits such as cutting, carving, moulding, weaving as well as singing, dancing, and cooking are capable of attaining technical excellence and fixed forms. The judgment of perfection of technical forms is essentially an aesthetic judgment. It is hardly possible to state objectively just where the line between artistic and pre-artistic forms should be drawn, because we cannot determine just where the aesthetic attitude sets in. It seems certain, however, that wherever a definite type has developed it must become a standard by which its perfection, that is, its beauty, is measured.

Although a mask is generally worn over the face, sometimes it covers almost the whole body of the wearer. It hides the identity of a person and with the help of its integral features, projects the wearer as another being. This indispensable characteristic of hiding and revealing moods or personalities is integral to all masks. As an important cultural element, masks have been used all over the world since the Paleolithic Period. However, masks found in different societies are varied in nature and in different societies they convey different symbols.

> Archaeologists study the relics of the past and, therefore, they can study only what has been preserved. Masks are usually made of perishable materials, wood, cloth, skin, fabric, nets, bark cloth (tapas), and such organic materials are rarely preserved for centuries. Luckily our early ancestors, modestly named as *Homo sapiens,* had the gift of producing art and among the subjects they have depicted in the walls of the rocks and caves there are depiction of masks. From that we learn that since 40,000 to 50,000 years ago our ancestors used to make and wear mask (Anati and Anati, 2001: 107).

With only a few exceptions, the morphological features of masks are derived from natural forms. Masks, which possess human features, are known as anthropomorphic, and those with animal features are known as theriomorphic. However, there are some masks which are the combination of anthropomorphic and theriomorphic features. Some of the masks closely resemble real objects while some others are made on the basis of imagination. Usually, masks represent demons and deities, ancestors, animals, imagined figures, etc. Among the uses of masks socio-religious, festive, theatrical, funerary, commemorative, and therapeutic uses, etc. are very common. From the prehistoric periods masks are used till today for various purposes. Masks have long been used by the militaries, sportsmen in some of the sports, divers, fire brigades, etc. Masks have been designed in innumerable varieties from a good number of materials available in the environment. Mask makers have shown great resourcefulness in selecting and combining the available materials in their surroundings. Among the materials used to make masks, bamboo, cane, clay, cloth, feather, fibre, fruit shell, leather, metal, paper, pith plant (*Aeschynomene indica*), stone, shell, wood, etc. are very common. Usually, the masks are made from perishable materials which are rarely preserved for centuries.

> The earliest example of masks are the representations of masked human figures found in paintings on rock-shelters which have been placed in the Mesolithic; besides, there are also examples of masked figures which are variously placed between the Mesolithic and the Historic Period. Apart of these, one also comes across what have been called the 'mascoids' engraved on rocks. It has been suggested that some of these masks could be considered as archetypes of later mask (Pande, 2001: 110).

Masks are generally worn with a costume; sometimes, such a costume is so complete that it covers the entire body of the wearer. With a particular mask a particular set of garb is worn. Without the specified type of costumes, the meaning and symbol of mask is not completed. The costume completes the new identity of the wearer. Like the masks costumes are also made from a good number of materials, and those have indispensable symbolic relation to the mask. A mask is not only a material object, but a device to appease or threat demons and deities, and by wearing it people try to get rid of hindrances in life, and to achieve pleasure and prosperity. Generally, masks are not made by all the members, but only by a few experts of society. It is believed in some of the societies that the mask makers felt the presence of the spirit while preparing a mask. It is also believed that some of the masks are the abode of the spirits, due to which in almost all the societies a good number of taboos are associated with masks.

Masks are generally found in two forms—tangible or rigid mask and pliant mask. Tangible masks can be separated from the face or the body of a person. This type of mask is made from a good number of materials, generally available in the environment of a community. The other type of mask is pliant mask. It is a type of mask which is not made from any material object but generally drawn over the face of a person. Laude (1971: 143) opines:

> Facial paintings, erased after the ceremony, may rightly be considered as belonging, to the general category of masks, no matter what their function, which varies from one group to another, may be. Since facial paintings are ephemeral, limited to the duration of the dance, they must be distinguished from anything that constitutes a permanent modification of outward appearance, such as tatooing, scarification, or dental filing. The latter transformations should be considered as a part of cosmetics, for they do not emerge directly from traditions associated with masks. The mask represents other beings with human support, whereas permanent physical alterations place a particular individual in his social and worldly framework.

The mask has an integral relation with performing arts found in a good number of backward and progressive societies. Even today, in some of the pristine rituals of the Europeans, tangible masks are used. Pliant masks represent usually malevolent and occasionally benevolent deities sanctioned by the culture. In different performing arts of innumerable societies, pliant masks are used. In Kathakali, a dance drama, and Koodiattam, a temple theatre of Kerala, pliant masks are indispensable. Among some of the African tribes pliant masks are traditionally popular. In India, Kerala has a notable tradition of pliant masks. Such masks are part and parcel of the Mudiyettu, Teyyan, and Yakshagana, three performing arts of that state.

Through the Mudiyettu ritual, the people appease goddess Bhadrakali, the ferocious and benevolent goddess, who killed the turbulent demon Darika. In the appeasement of Bhadrakali, which is generally held in Travancore and Kochin regions, Mudiyettu dance dramas are invariably performed. In such performances, the faces of the performers are adorned with intricate designs made by different bright colours. Teyyam, Teyyattam, Tira, and Tirayattam, are folk performing arts still present in North Kerala to adore the traditional heroes and some of the deities. In such type of performances, pliant masks are used by the performers. Yakshagana is a very popular and living tradition of Kerala. Yaksha is a supernatural being, and believed to be superior to men and inferior to gods. Yakshagana literally means 'singing of Yaksha'. In this type of performing art, pliant masks are used by the performers.

Masks are usually used for three purposes. After wearing a mask, a person becomes a different creature. The mask hides his identity and reveals him as a different one. When he performs, he becomes an integral part of a ritual. In such a case, a mask becomes the medium of a demon or a deity. If a mask changes the wearer's outward features only, he becomes a part of a drama; a mask then becomes a stylized or symbolic face of a supernatural entity. Moreover, masks are also used by the cosmonauts, physicians, athletes, etc. to satisfy utilitarian purposes.

> In primitive cultures the mask is neither a symbol nor a metaphor but a tangible presence. Our analytical mind may qualify it as mythical presence, but for the primitives myth is a more intense reality. Therefore, for them masks are, as Seigfreid Giedion calls them, the antennae of invisible forces.
>
> In whatever way a mask is used, as a mythical presence, a symbol, a metaphor or as a protective clothing worn by twentieth-century cosmonauts, it would always be a way of defying human vulnerability' (Pani, 1986: 7).

Mask is a culture complex and a good number of elements are indispensably related to it in every society. The study of primitive art including mask has attracted many anthropologists and scholars from various disciplines. To quote Biebuyck (1969: 64):

> Thus in 1972 Boas presented a very modern view of the role of the artists in the shaping of given art style. Until then, the different styles of the primitive arts were mainly conceived of as technological trouvailles, engendered by the skills of weaving, painting, plaiting, chipping, chopping and such. It was believed that, in the course of time, these trouvailles were fused together in a rigid framework of stylistic convention and tradition. Inspired by Boas, Olbrechts was the first to formulate in detail the principles of modern ethno-aesthetic research. Curiously enough, very little has come from Olbrechts'

> viewpoint. Two of his students in 1938 went on an expedition to the Ivory Coast in West Africa to carry out research in line with Olbrechts' efforts. Unfortunately only a small part of their results has been made accessible in print.

Some of the communities have the heritage of making large masks. In Assam, the Vaishnavite people used to wear very big anthropomorphic, theriomorphic, masks in some of the rituals. The Papuans inhabited in New Guinea built very large masks known as *hevehe,* which are generally 20 feet in height. These are made from palm wood covered with bark cloth; they make eye-catching designs on it, and adorn the mask with painted cane stripes. It is believed that such large frightening masks protect people from all hazards and bring peace, joy, and prosperity. In India, a good number of communities have the tradition of mask making; some of them use masks till today for different purposes. However, archaeological evidence of masks in this country is scanty.

> The specimens available so far as miniature masks of terracotta which vary in dimensions but hardly ever of life-size, except for example of one from Chirand in district Chapra in Bihar and another from Rangmahal in district Rajasthan, and some examples of masks used as covering of human skull from Manipur...... (Pande, 2001: 110).

There is no prehistoric evidence to know about the past of the glorious tradition of mask in Assam. Till recent past, the craftsmen of Assam used to make masks from bamboo, clay, earthen pot, gourd shell, pith plant, sheath of areca nut leaf, wood, etc. Though wood and pith plant are used, nowadays the mask makers of Assam, particularly the mask makers of the *satras,* usually make masks from the bamboo split covered with cotton cloth, clay, and cow-dung. The craftsman who has to work with a stone or a wooden log has to often limit the size of the mask to that of the material used. On the other hand, the Vaishnavite craftsmen of Assam are in a better position, because they principally make mask with bamboo split, which can be easily moulded and shaped according to their ideas.

According to Vidyarthi (1993: 91),

> The Sherdukpen, the Khamba, and the Monpas (inhabitants of Arunachal Pradesh) are famous for their artistic creation. They prepare ornate dresses and large number of masks, which appear almost like real faces, while others represent birds and animals and some represent

apes and men with twisted mouths, women with goiter to drive away the evil spirit.

Elwin commented on the masks of Arunachal Pradesh as follows:

> The masks are made of a single block of wood hollowed inside; holes are usually, but not always, made for eyes and mouths; most masks are painted, but older ones are generally found dark and discoloured. The paints are brought from Tibet or the Assam plains. Women never wear the mask, which are used only by men and boys and in Tawang (Arunachal Pradesh), by Lamas themselves (cited in Vidyarthi, 1993: 91).

Assam has a rich heritage of masks. Till today, masks are used in different folk performing art of Assam. As for example in the *Kusan gan* and *Bhari gan* of undivided Goalpara district of Assam, uses of masks are indispensable. In the *Khulia bhaoria*, another folk performing art of Darrang district, also masks are used. It is pertinent to note that all these three types of performing art are usually based on the stories of the *Ramayana* and the *Mahabharata*, where no written scripts are used. Instead, the actors portray a story of the said Hindu scriptures using their spontaneous dialogues. In these art forms, only the male take part; the female characters are also performed by the male members. In such performances, for depicting the characters of demons, deities, serpents, imaginary creatures, etc. the actors generally wear different types of masks. Usually, masks are worn to express ferocity and other feelings which are not possible to express by human beings with bare faces. According to Bouissac (2001: 73),

> The natural transformations of the face in social interactions comprise at least three types:
>
> 1. Muscular contractions (of the superficial skeletal muscles) that create patterns through the interplay of relief's and shadows. These are mostly under voluntary control.
> 2. Circulatory regulations that modify the shape of erectile vascular tissues (such as the lower eyelids and the lips) and the colour of the facial skin (for instance the cheeks and the lips). These may become somewhat under voluntary control through training.
> 3. Neuroautomatisms that are under the control of the autonomic nervous system (such as the enlargement of the pupils at the centre of the eye when the person is in a state of arousal). These totally escape voluntary control and can be voluntarily modified only through artifices.

In each society, there is pristine permission and prohibition integral to facial expressions. In all cultures, keen attention has been paid to train the members about the facial expression according to the context. Some of the facial expressions are taken as the sign of vulgarity and bad manner of a person. Moreover, an expression accepted in a particular situation like in marriage ceremony, different festivals, etc. is not accepted in a mortuary rite or in some other rituals. The facial expressions tabooed in different environments of a culture are also depicted through the masks made by the members of that society. This proves that masks are the medium through which one can express such feelings which do not have social sanction.

In most of the societies, tradition restricts the imagination of a mask maker, and he is not allowed to make a mask ignoring the pristine code. There are many tales about the harassment by demons and deities to the mask maker for creating a mask ignoring the traditional strictures. Moreover, such masks create displeasure amongst the fellow members of the society. It should be noted that in almost all the societies, mask making is a male job. In Assam, although it is not tabooed for the women, yet all the mask makers of the state are males only. A mask maker creates a mask within the traditional framework; the spectators of the society can explain every feature of a mask, because they are also acquainted with the norms and values of the society. While wearing a mask, it is believed that the person feels the presence of the demon or deity who lives in the mask, in his body and heart. Some of the masks are greatly revered by the people and only pious and good men are allowed to wear such masks. There are many stories of mishappening due to the wearing of revered mask by a wicked person camouflaging his mischievous activities. Sometimes, the wearer of a mask undergoes a psychic change and behaves like the demon whose mask he has worn and foretells in a frenzy. A paramount role of mask is to provide the change of the age of the demon or the deity and to correlate it with the present time. The spectators of a particular society can easily identify the different masks, and the gestures and postures of the wearer because they are the bearers of the same culture. A mask can create pleasure and gaiety; however, most of the masks create fear, anguish, and death. Monte (1969: 9) writes,

> The mask does not depict a single emotion at a particular time, it is not a portrait of a man who fears, who fights or who dies; it is a symbol of fear, war, and death.

It has been already stated that masks represent various feelings, particularly integral to day-to-day experiences by the members of a society. Roy (1985: 58) writes,

> The faces with their varied types of expression fear, sorrow, etc.- freeze to reflect the universal experiences that serve as a fountain of recreation; they also act as a medium to reckon the past events primarily related to the legends. This travels across the barrier of time and space, although its effect is relative to time and space. In the plains (of Assam) the masks primarily become associated with the legends of greater Indian classical tradition while in Arunachal Pradesh (specially among the Monpas), they become compounded with the Buddhist tradition that travels through Tibet. These traditions have their profound impact upon the modelling of the masks. Each and every stroke of the chisel of the craftsman while carving out the face is dictated by the cultural codes of the milieu to which the craftsman belongs. In the case of wooden mask, the artist has to work with the wooden log that poses him a limitation. The size and shape of the log condition the dimension of the mask. But the craftsman with his given appliance gives it a vivid expression. In this respect the craftsman working with clay and basketry is in a more comfortable condition.

> Masks are part of our being, their making and use are expressions of human nature, like showing off is part of the nature of a peacock. Masks imply the will or need of producing a reality that provides the power of pertinent behaviour. Our species has the need to create the appropriate image in order to act according to the alternative realities. Masks have the same roles and motivations of many other daily actions of man (Anati and Anati, 2001: 108).

Physical structure of the masks are extraordinarily varied; likewise their fundamental meaning and functions are also immensely different in nature. Laude (1971: 148-175) categorized masks of Africa in the following types:

I. Leaf and wooden mask, which also includes grass mask
II. Facial mask
III. Helmet mask
IV. Helmet-shaped mask
V. Blade-shaped mask
VI. Mask crown by sculptures

The universe of the mask is the world of imagination. In some of the backward societies and also in some comparatively progressive societies, masks are mainly associated with ceremonies and festivals which have social and religious significance. Masks are also used with funerary rituals, to cure disease and ailments, in fertility rights and so on. Use of masks in performing arts like plays, dance drama, etc. is very common in a good number of societies. Today, masks are used in some of the sports and also in warfare.

3.2 USES OF MASK

Masks have an intricate existence in the socio-cultural matrix of different societies and have been used for different purposes, among which socio-religious uses are overwhelming. Some of the principal uses of mask are given below:

3.2 (A) Disciplinary Uses

Masks are sometimes used for maintaining discipline. They are also used to admonish children, criminals, and women. Some of the masks are so big that they completely cover the body of the wearers; such masks are found in Africa, China, North America, Oceania, etc. Such masks create fear in people's mind and help to control the society. Some of the African Negro tribes strongly believe that the first mask was an admonitory one. To restrict a child from disturbing thew mother in the mundane duties, sometimes a few African tribes use ferocious looking masks in some of their implements. As for example, a child while following his or her mother in fetching water is frightened by a hideous face drawn on the bottom of the mother's pitcher prepared from bottle gourd.

3.2 (B) To Maintain Status

Mask is an object which exhibits close relation with all three environments—geographical, social, and magico-religious. Mask has a close relation to the norms and values of a society, and in some of the societies it is the medium through which the status and prestige of a person are measured. Through a mask, a society communicates with the supernaturals. A priest or a shaman wearing a mask becomes a deity. In many cultures all through the world, a judge wears a mask to hide his identity and also to protect him from recriminations; it is believed that through the mask he is possessed by a spirit who assumes responsibility for the decision levied on the culprit. In some of the societies, some persons have to use masks while performing some activities.

3.2(c) Use in Initiation

Masks are invariably used in the initiation ritual by a good number of tribes, particularly in Africa. Among some African tribes, when a young member is admitted to the secret society, they usually conduct the rituals of initiation; in such rituals the new member is instructed about his future role for controlling the socio-cultural balance of the tribe. Totemic and spiritualistic masks are donned by the elder members in such rituals. Among some African Negro tribes of West Coast, intricately carved impressive human masks are found, which are used in the ritual of initiation. In Africa, particularly in western and central Congo Kinshasa, huge colourful helmet-like masks are used as a masquerading device when the youths return from the initiation area and are introduced to the villagers as adult members of the tribe. As for example among the Pende tribe of Africa, distinctive colourful masks are given to the youths who have been initiated, and by wearing them they have to go through a prolonged ordeal of training and initiation rites. After the ritual such masks are cast aside and replaced by small and symbolic ivory duplicate, which are the symbols of their manhood, and believed to protect them from all misfortunes.

3.2 (d) To Appease Ancestors and Deities

Myths and masks are indispensably related.

> Even today, tribes and communities which have been least influenced by industrial civilization perform mask rituals. The priests wearing the masks become gods. Here a kind of double metamorphosis takes place: the mask, psychologically elevates the wearer to influence the supernatural powers to which he appeals and at the same time permits them to transfigure him. He then acquires psychic substance from supernatural powers and passes this on to the members of his community or tribe. Mask rituals, often accompanied by powerful percussive music and solemn singing, lead to states of collective hysteria. The participants believe that the ritual forces supernatural powers to put in an appearance. The magic spell of the ritual is not limited only to the wearer of masks; all the participants of the ceremony feel the presence of the divine beings summoned by the magic power of the mask (Pani, 1986: 2).

Worshipping of ancestors is a common custom among many tribes of the world. A good number of tribes of Africa, China, etc. communicate with their forefathers and pray for well-being by performing rites and wearing masks. In the western part of Melanesia, large varieties of ancestral masks are found which vary greatly in materials and styles. The Sepik River area in North Central New Guinea is the place extremely rich in ancestral masks ranging from a small facial to a gigantic mask. These masks are carved out from wood and the affixed appendages like animal's skin, feathers, fibres, flowers, seeds, shells, etc. make those masks different from each other. Usually, the masks are coloured with earth colours of red and yellow, lime white, and charcoal black. These masks have both social and religious significance and often they represent ancestors as well as malevolent spirits.

Among the North-West Coast, of North America, a peculiar type of mask is found. Some parts of such mask are detachable and after detaching those a second face is revealed, generally that of a human image. The inhabitants of the area strongly believe that a human spirit could take the form of an animal, bird, reptile, etc. and vice versa. Detachable masks are made by them on this concept. Through some of these articulating masks they depict some of the lores and tales in different rituals. 'The role of the mask is to reaffirm, at regular intervals, the truth and the immediate presence of myths in everyday life. Masks strengthen the collective existence in all its complex aspects' (Laude: 1971).

3.2 (E) In Secret Society

It is believed that masks are invented by a secret society of Africa to hide one's identity while punishing a murderer. In New Britain, members of the terrorist secret society known as *dukduk* used to wear around 5-foot long monstrous masks while appearing before police, judge, and to execute offenders. Such masks are made from a good number of materials like bark cloth, pith of certain reed, etc. These masks are painted in bright colours, predominantly by green and brick red colours. Aggressive malevolent spirits are represented by such masks. Nocturnal rituals observed by the members of the secret societies generally wear ancestor masks. In Assam also, there are nocturnal secret societies, though the members of such a society do not use masks while performing the secret ritual (*rati seva*). In West Africa and along the Guinea Coast, many stylized and realistic ancestor masks are used by the members of the secret societies, each of which has some specific cultural role, and such a mask determines the power and prestige of the wearer. The structure and forms and also uses of the mask are invariably determined by the tradition. It is worth mentioning that innumerable masks are found among different tribes of Africa, which exhibit a wide range of thought-provoking varieties. A good number of masks are integral to the secret societies of Africa.

3.2 (F) Funerary and Commemorative Uses

In many of the societies mortuary rites, particularly the burial customs are very important, and in some such societies masks are used to represent a dead and the departing spirits. Funerary masks are generally anthropomorphic in form, which are used to cover the face of the deceased. Such a mask represents the features of the dead, and also establishes a relationship with the spirit world. It is believed that such a mask protects the deceased by frightening the evil spirits, and also compel the dead man's spirit to leave the world and to proceed towards the spirit world. The ancient Egyptians from the Middle Kingdom, *c.* 2040-1786 BC to the first century AD, placed the mask on the face of the deceased which possessed the features of the dead. These masks were generally made of cloth covered with stucco or plaster, and finally painted. It was believed that these masks lead the person to the resting place of the soul. The most splendid burial mask was made in c. 1350 BC for the cremation of Pharaoh Tutankhamen. For the important persons, generally masks of gold and silver were made. Gold masks were also used to cover the faces of the dead kings of Cambodia and Siam.

In Egypt, mummies of lesser personages were often covered with masks made of clay or wood. The faces of the mummies of Inca royalty were generally covered by gold masks. Some ancient Andean metallic death masks possessed movable parts. In the Moon pyramid at Moche of Peru, a mask is found with movable ears. The ancient burial masks of the Mexicans seem to be generic representations rather than the depiction of the features of the deceased. During the 1st and 2nd centuries AD, a type of mask had been produced in the Fayyam region of Egypt. Such masks were made during the lifetime of a person as realistic portraits painted in encaustic on wood. When a person dies, such a mask is used to cover his face. Death masks were sometimes preserved by the patrician families of Rome as ancestors' portraits and were displayed on ceremonial occasions. Generally, such masks were made of wax and represented the physical features of the dead. From the Middle Ages through the 18th century, effigy masks used by the royalty and nobility of Europe were made in the same technique following patrician families of Rome.

'Through masks and figures many societies keep touch with their dead. Among the most striking of the African funeral masks are those used by the Maw society of the Ibo tribe in Nigeria. White paint, representing the spirit of the dead, enhances the skeletal features of the mask. Deceased ancestors communicate with the living during the funeral dances in which these masks are used' (Conrad, 1967: 215). The skull masks of the Aztecs are generally used in funerary rites, and like their wooden masks, were inlaid with mosaics of lignite and turquoise, while eye sockets were adorned with pyrites. In Melanesia, a mask is made of clay, resin, or wax, which represents the features of a person's head/ skull, which is meticulously painted and designed. A man can wear such masks in his lifetime, and in his death it is used to cover his face during the funerary rite.

3.2 (G) Totemic Uses

The concept of totem is common among many tribes of the world. Some communities observe elaborate rituals and observe a good number of taboos to appease their totems. Sometimes they use masks to please the totems. The African totem masks have highly polished surface, which are generally carved from hard wood and designed with graceful lines. In Western Africa, beautifully designed elongated animal masks are very common. In New Ireland and New Caledonia masks are usually prepared from wood, dried grass, coconut-shells, fibre, etc. These masks generally possess distorted exaggerated features of animals, birds, fishes, etc. Believing everything in nature is possessed by a spirit, man found authority for himself, his family, or for his clan, by identifying with a specific non-human spirit. He adopted usually an animal and tried mythologically to trace his ancestry from that animal. He preempted the animal as the symbol and authority of himself, his family, lineage, and clan. Such an animal is known as totem, though in some societies non-animal totem like tree, cosmic body, etc. are also found. In many societies of the world, where there is the concept of totem, making of totem's mask is a common practice. They believe that by wearing such masks they can overcome the obstacles of life, and the specific totem will bring comfort and prosperity for them. Among some of the tribes the medicine man, principal priest, shaman, etc. generally wear the very effective and powerful totem masks, and it is believed that such masks could exorcise malevolent spirits, locate animals and fish, cure diseases and ailments, predict weather, and punish the enemies.

3.2 (h) Therapeutic Uses

In many societies masks have played a notable role in preventing and curing diseases and ailments. It is a known fact that masks are integral to magico-religious practices in different cultures. In some cultures, the members of the secret societies drive away demons and deities, who are supposed to have caused particular diseases, by wearing mask and dancing or shouting and making specific gestures. Members of the False Face Society, a secret society of the Iroquois Indians inhabiting North America, drive away the spirits and deities who cause diseases through mask dance. These members of the secret society are regarded as professional healers among the Iroquois, and they perform vigorous pantomimes to exorcise the notorious and trickful demon Gahadogoka Gogosa, who plagued the Iroquois. The dreadful masks worn by them are embellishments of different natural objects over the long wigs made of the hair of horse tail.

To emphasize the grotesqueness of mask, sometimes metallic inserts were used around the eyes. In some societies masks are used to prevent diseases. Among the Sinhalese of Sri Lanka, around twenty masks are identified which were used by them to prevent and cure different diseases. These fanged and ferocious looking masks are sometimes adorned with animal jaws and have startling eyes. Among the Chinese, during the epidemics of cholera children are protected through cholera masks. They also use masks to protect the faces of their children from measles.

Probably, the earliest mask was used in hunting. In the early Stone Age Period, disguise masks were used for the success of hunting, and it was believed that these masks help to placate the animal's spirit after slaughtering. In the cave arts of Trois Freres in Ariege, France, the so-called sorcerer is seen with a disguise mask. The animal mask worn by Altaic and Tungusic shamans exhibit close relations to that of the sorcerer of the cave art of France.

From time immemorial, masks have been used in military purposes. These masks are hideously fantastic features and generally have ferocious expression to infuse fear among the enemies. A kind of ludicrous mask helmet known as *menpo* was used by the Japanese *samurais*. The Chinese and the Roman warriors adorn their shields with grotesque and grimacing masks. Sometimes they used masks to their armour to terrify the enemies. In many sports, masks are used. The horsemen of the Roman army used symbolic and decorative masks to protect their head, face, arms, etc. The workers of fire brigade and the divers also use masks to protect their body parts.

3.2 (I) Theatrical Uses

Theatrical performances are a visual art of a transient and momentary nature where masks have been almost universally used to represent characters. By wearing a mask an actor reveals him as a real character.

> Of the mask used for some kind of theatrical or some other similar purposes, the specimens from Chirand and Rangmahal provide good examples. Both these belong to the Early Historic Period and are life-size unlike the Harappan examples which are miniature in size. As suggested by us earlier, there is every possibility of the practice of making masks of less durable material which have not survived. The death mask from Manipur were of gold as well as of copper and were used as covering the human skull as part of some mortuary rites (Pande, 2001: 119).

In many performing arts of India, masks are indispensable. As for example in the fascinating Chhau dance prevalent in Bihar, Orissa, and West Bengal, masks are used. Though Chhau is generally regarded as a dance form, in close scrutiny it reveals that it is more of a form of theatre than a dance. It should be noted here that in different performing arts, the actors use both tangible and pliant masks. The masks have a close relation with myths. The mask as an important part of theatre first emerged in western civilization from the religious practices of the ancient Greece. In the appeasing ritual of the Dionysus, the god of fecundity and good crop, some of the devotees used to wear goat skins and imbibed wine, which eventually developed into the sophistication of masking. In some of the rituals, they used to wear masks to make the god manifest.

Pani writes (1986: 16-17),

> One of the most important devices is the treatment of the actor's face by elaborate make-up in different colours and designs and also through

use of masks. In almost all type of masks used in traditional theatre, the headgear forms an integral part of the mask and there is an amazing range and variety of headgears in both material and design. The mask-makers use a variety of materials such as clay, wood, bark, cork, pith, hide, tapestry, bamboo, papier mache, etc. The masks are of different sizes from the small masks of Seraikela Chhau to the huge ones of Sahi Jatra of Orissa and Krishnattam of Kerala. Most of the masks are in one piece, but some have moving parts. Some are carved, others painted, while some are both carved and painted. Masks representing gods, human beings, animals and demons have been treated with a variety of interpretations. The masks also demonstrate a great range of colour schemes and designs. The idea of colour symbolism is often followed as in the case of the make-up in Kathakali.

Among many tribes of Arunachal Pradesh, masks are related to different dimensions of life; however, the use of masks in theatrical performances are principally related to the Buddhist tribes. The Khamba, the Monpa, and the Sherdukpen use colourful masks made of wood in theatrical performances. It has already been mentioned that in many folk performances of Assam, masks are invariably used. The Rabha and the Bodo tribes of Brahmaputra plains of Assam also traditionally use masks in different folk performances.

Theatrical performances originating in Greece saw masks being used for portraying different ages, occupations, personalities, and ranks. The Greek actors used gigantic masks made of leather and painted canvas to depict mythological characters. In the Middle Ages, during the 12th to 16th century, masks were used in mystery plays based on Old and New Testaments. In such performances, devils, demons, dragons, and the characters who did seven deadly sins were represented by wearing grotesque masks. No reliable records of such masks are found. It is believed that these were made of papier-mache which could belch fire and smoke from the hidden contrivances. Such masks are still used in Alpine Austria to represent demons and deities in different carnivals.

During the Renaissance of 15th century in Italy, theatrical performances spread to England, France, and also to Germany. The Roman comic dramas were performed in those places depicting the mundane life of the people where masks were extensively used. Generally, these ludicrous masks were made of leather. Fortunately, excellent pictorial records of such masks are present. During the 18th to 20th centuries, except in comedy plays in the form of puppet and marionette shows, masks disappeared from western theatre. In modern revivals of ancient Greek drama, masks are occasionally used symbolically. In the traditional *No* dramas of Japan, masks play an important role. Among the Japanese, there are 125 classified varieties of masks divided into five categories—devils, goblins, gods, goddesses, and old persons—both male and female. These masks are made of wood with a coating of plaster, which is gilded and lacquered and made bright by using traditional colours.

Sacred dramas performed by the *lamas* and the priests of Tibet invariably use awe-inspiring masks to represent demons and deities. A play known as 'Dance of the Red Tiger Devil' is performed annually for exorcizing demons where masks made of cloth, papier-mache, and occasionally gilt copper are used. In the Indian states of Bhutan and Sikkim wood is abundant, and the inhabitants of both the states carved masks from durable wood. The Himalayan people generally used the wooden masks adorned with coloured wigs made of yak tail. Such masks create a hideous environment in the ritualistic performances of the Himalayan region. Like the *Kabuki* actors of Japan, in the secular dramas of China pliant masks made by cosmetics and paints are used. Such a mask marks the features of a particular actor and his personality.

The strictly sacred dramas of China are performed by the actors wearing grotesque and fanciful masks. Masks are also used in congratulatory playlets, dance dramas, pageants, and processions in China with elaborate head-gears and other ornaments. In the dragon and lion dances of China and Japan, the mask dancers move to the taps of a small drum. The lower jaw of such a mask is movable and by means of a string made to emit loud and continuous clacking. In Bali and Java, *Wayang Wong*, a kind of traditional play, performed by the masked actors. The stories of such plays are based on Sanskrit scriptures. These are not only performed for amusement but also to overcome the barriers and misfortunes of life by appeasing gods. The *Wayang Wong* is developed from the shadow puppet plays of the 18th century. These masks are generally made of wood and leather and often adorned with horse hair and gilded or metallic accoutrements.

In some of the Vaishnavite rituals of Assam, masks are indispensable. These masks are the part of *Bhakti* movement without any touch of magical fervour. It should be noted here that *Ankiya bhaona,* i.e., the Vaishnavite one-act play, is integral to Assamese Vaishnavism.

Principally, in the *Ankiya bhaonas* (one act Vaishnavite play) and also in different theatrical performances of the Vaishnavite institutions, many mythological characters are integral and to express the features and feelings of such mythological characters masks are worn. At present, masks are also sometimes used by some of the characters of modern drama and dance drama.

3.2 (J) Other Uses

Masks are also used to celebrate seasons.

> Ceremonies in which masks are exhibited are usually agrarian rituals or funerals. These ceremonies are spectacles in which music, chanting, and measured recitation of mythical poems form a broad dynamic and colourful choreographic ensemble, played out over several days in the public square. The initiated serve as actors and the spectators are those villagers who are not bound by any prohibitions, temporary or permanent. The wearing of masks is generally a male prerogative; women are not allowed to see them. In societies such as the Mende in Sierra Leone, however, there exist strictly feminine ceremonies (Laude, 1971: 139).

Masks are also used by the masqueraders. The Kalahari Ijo, inhabitants of the delta area of Nigeria, invoked Ekine spirits, their cult gods, during the dry season of the year. Ekines are the water spirits; they are not invoked for the general benefits like health, wealth, peace, prosperity, etc., but for the success of play, which the masquerades perform for entertainment. To portray some of the characters in such plays, the masqueraders sometimes wear masks. Such a performer 'may be remembered by his aptitude as a dancer in a particular mask of the play. A miniature replica of his mask will be placed on his ancestor memorial and his heirs will inherit the right to dance in that mask or a whole play that he introduced' (Duerden, 1970: 17). In the Egungum cult of the Yoruba in Nigeria, appeasing the ancestors is an indispensable part of the religion. In the sacred festivals, to propitiate the ancestors the hereditary chief of the Egungum secret societies chooses a man to wear a mask. When he is wearing the mask, it is believed that he is possessed by the spirit. After wearing the mask the man ceases to speak in his normal voice and instead he speaks in the voice of the ancestor's spirit whose mask he wears. 'Horton, in an article in *Nigeria* magazine, has described how the Ekine masqueraders stage a graduation ceremony. If a new member fails to carry out the steps correctly then his mask will be taken from him by a rival house of masqueraders; those who have failed in this way have been known in the past to commit suicide' (Duerden, 1970: 19). Among many tribes, masks are used by the group dancers to celebrate the season. Different seasons like dry, cold, etc. are observed by a good number of African tribes through dancing. In such ceremonies, sometimes masks are worn by the dancers. Sometimes, masks are used by the 'leopard man' of the Aniotas, a dreaded sect of Congo; they also use masks in dances preceding military campaigns.

4

Heritage of Mask at Majuli

4.1 MASK MAKING TRADITION

Majuli has a praiseworthy tradition of mask making. In the remote past, it is said by many old men of Natun Chamaguri Satra, a loud voice of unknown being was heard from the river Brahmaputra urging people to learn a skill as *'Banhtote kathito, jopatote pachito'*, the meaning of which is 'you will get a piece of split from a bamboo and a basket from a bamboo grove'. The miraculous voice was heard again and again to inspire the people of Majuli for learning the skill of mask making. The primary occupation of the people of Majuli is agriculture and they are all bound to the wheel of agricultural works. The other works like basketry, boat making, domestication of animals, etc. are more or less an obligation to them. Therefore, nobody intended whole-heartedly to obey the voice and to learn the skill of mask making. They also thought that they will get only a split from a bamboo and a basket only from a bamboo grove. During that period, baskets and such articles were not commodities for sale in market. Hand fan (*bichani)*, different types of baskets like *pachi, kharahi, don,* etc. are made by the persons who know the skill, and generally such articles were taken by the co-villagers without giving any money to the maker. Owing to such a situation, the people of Majuli had not shown any inclination towards learning the new craft.

It is a known fact that no society can work throughout the year without any recreational activities. In Assam in general and in Majuli in particular also, there are many recreational activities knitted to the agricultural cycle when strenuous activities stopped for a few days or ended for the season. In such periods they performed many recreational activities, which gave them hope and energy to struggle with the uncongenial environment of the riverine island. Among these recreational activities, folk theatrical performances are important. In such performances they used masks made from different materials like clay, earthen pitcher, sheath of areca nut leaves, wood, etc. Even today some very old wooden masks are found in different *satras* of Majuli.

Sankaradeva, the renowned saint of 15th century, had initiated and propagated Vaishnavism in North-East India. In his venture Majuli occupied an important place. He established the first *satra* at Duvahat Belguri of Majuli. *Satra* is not only a centre for the propagation of religion but also an educational centre to learn different skills indispensable for living in a community. Moreover, theatrical performances are integral to the religious activities of Assam's Vaishnavism. Srimanta Sankaradeva was a versatile genius, and he was famed to be adept in various skills like making of drum, mask, and other articles necessary for Vaishnavism and also maintenance of day-to-day life. It is believed that the great saint had innovated the technique of making mask from bamboo splits with varied types of expressions like fear, joy, sorrow, vigour, pride, happiness, etc. These masks acted as the medium to present the events described in the Vaishnavite scriptures to the people with a great precision, and thus they became instruments of recreation and religious teaching. Soon it developed as an important craft of the area and travelled across the barriers of time and space. In old days, it is known that, in many of the *satras* of Majuli mask making became an important craft. There are two types of *satras* in Majuli; in one type the *satradhikar* and the *bhaktas* can marry, and in the other type they remain celibates. However, in a celibate *satra* also if a *bhakta* desires he can take the permission from the *satradhikar* and the congregation of *bhaktas* to lead a conjugal life. It is pertinent to note here that a *satra* is the abode of the males only and the females are strictly prohibited to live in it. Generally, a male child from a poor family whose parents are not capable of smoothly maintaining the household, offers the child to a *satra*. In some families, where a mother suffers from still-birth repeatedly, or the new born babies die one after another, she may take a vow to offer her unborn child to a *satra.* Due to such reasons, many small boys of different ages are seen in a celibate (*udasin) satra.* Such boys are trained in different skills practised in a *satra.* A *satra,* which has the tradition of mask making, is taught to these teenagers.

A *satra* may have the tradition of mask making or not, but each *satra* has to use masks in some of their rituals and festivals. The *satras* which do not have the tradition of mask making used to bring masks from the *satras* where the skill was practised. At present there are only four *satras* in Majuli, viz., Alengi Narasimha, Bihimpur, Natun Chamaguri, and Prachin Chamaguri, where mask making is a living tradition. It should be noted here that in all these four *satras, satradhikars* are married persons.

4.2 MAKING OF MASK

To make a mask, the craftsman uses a local variety of bamboo known as *jatibanh (Bambusa tulda Roxb),* which is neither immature nor very mature. First with the help of a machete (*da*), the bamboo is cut into pieces of about 2 to 2.5 metre in length. These bamboo pieces are kept in pond water or pool for a period of 5 to 7 days. The soaking of bamboo pieces in water prevents insect attack and provides more flexibility to the bamboo tubes. Then, with the machete the tubes are longitudinally cut into a few pieces from which splits are made with the help of a sharp knife (*katari*). These bamboo splits are woven in open hexagonal pattern to make the base of the mask. 'In hexagonal work the wefts instead of being horizontal and vertical are worked in three directions, forming in open work hexagonal spaces in close work, six pointed star' (A committee of Royal Anthropological Institute of Great Britain and Ireland, 1954: 273). Use of open hexagonal pattern as a basketry technique in Assam is very old. The mask makers referred to this as *Lakhimi sutra.* Lakhimi or Lakshmi is the Hindu goddess of wealth and prosperity. Goddess Lakshmi is also known by the name Sri, which means 'beauty'. A mask is an object of beauty and the epitome of aesthetic value. Moreover, throughout Assam paddy seeds for sowing are preserved cautiously in a bamboo basket (*tom*), which is invariably weaved in an open hexagonal pattern. Irrespective of caste and creed, the Assamese people respect paddy as one of the abodes of goddess Lakshmi. Among all the baskets integral to paddy cultivation, only *tom* is weaved in open hexagonal pattern. Because the mask is weaved like a *tom* and the *tom* is believed to be the abode of goddess Lakshmi or Lakhimi, therefore, the weaving *sutra* (definition) of the mask is known as *Lakhimi sutra.*

The woven base of a mask is covered with one or more pieces of old cotton fabrics, which are wiped with a paste of a special type of clay *(Kumarmati)* and water before covering the mask. It should be noted that among the Hindus, cow-dung is a sacred object which is invariably used to sanctify a place or a person. However, in making of mask cow-dung is not used as an ingredient for its sacredness but for its stickiness. It is said by the mask makers that the dung of the calves who live only on their mother's milk possessed more adhesive power than that of an adult cow. Then a mixture is made with the ingredients like the cow-dung of calves, clay, and water is applied over the mask for a few times according to the requirement. In this step, features of the mask become prominent. This step is known as *chehera dia,* which means 'giving the appearance'. Then it is dried in sunshine. Before completely drying, the mask is scrapped with a bamboo scraper *(karani),* which is followed by drying and colouring of the mask. Embellishments like hair, moustache, crown, and required ornaments are finally added to a mask.

In olden days, the craftsmen used natural colours for the beautification of a mask which were extracted from various natural objects. *Hengul* (red colour) and *haital* (the yellow orpiment) are extracted from natural ores. The black colour is prepared from the ashes of the cooking pots or from the smoke of kerosene lamps; green colour is derived from crushing different leaves, and white colour is extracted from a kind of soil *(dhal mati),* generally found at a depth of 1½ mt from the surface of the earth. Red colour is also derived from *achu gach/daru haridra* (*Morinda angustifolia* Roxb). The gum to attach hair and moustaches, etc. is prepared from the fruits of *kotkora (M. spinosa* Roxb. ex Link), *bihmana* (*Randia spinosa*), bel (*Aegle marmelos*), or *kendu (Diospyros embryopteris),* while hair and moustaches were generally prepared from water hyacinth, locally known as *pani meteka* (*Eichhornia crassipes*), or from jute fibre, locally known as *marapat*. Embellishment are prepared from tin-foil (*rang pata*) and coloured papers. Extraction of natural colour is a very painstaking, time-consuming, and strenuous process. Therefore, nowadays the craftsmen use colours available in the market. They also buy easily available different bright objects to prepare ornaments, etc. However, till today they generally prepare hair and moustaches from jute fibre although sometimes they use synthetic fibres also to make them. During the pre-independent period, craftsmen kept colours in bamboo tubes of different sizes; small brushes were made from pigeons' feathers or bamboo sticks by adding goat's hair as bristles; broad brushes were made by fixing jute fibre to bamboo sticks. Today, the mask makers use synthetic brushes. However, till today each craftsman uses pristine broad brushes made of jute fibre and bamboo stick.

While moulding the faces of demoness Surpanakha (sister of Ravana), Narasimha (an incarnation of Vishnu), etc., the craftsman strictly abides by the description of the features given in the scriptures. That is why the mask of Narasimha (man-lion) made at Majuli closely resembles a horse than a lion. According to Roy (1984-85: 58),

> The faces with their varied types of expression—fear, sorrow, etc., freeze to reflect the universal experiences that serve as fountain of recreation: they also act as a medium to reckon the past events primarily related to legends. This travels across the barrier of time and space, although its effects are relative to time and space.

Sri Hemchandra Goswami, aged 53 years, a renowned mask maker of Natun Chamaguri Satra, said that during his childhood he has seen the extraction of colours from various natural objects. His father, late Rudrakanta Deva Goswami, was the *satradhikar* of Natun Chamaguri Satra. Late Deva Goswami was well known for his expertise in mask making throughout undivided Assam. Many reputed art critics of the state acclaimed the works of late Deva Goswami. During his childhood, Sri Goswami saw how his father prepared various colours from natural objects. Sri Goswami opines that the natural colours are very bright and last for a longer period. He said that nowadays these objects are not easily available in the river island Majuli. Due to the repeated floods and for the growing population, the jungles have been transformed into habitats. Moreover, in Majuli generally the people frequently change their village in search of comparatively high land to get rid of the turbulent flood. Due to these reasons, nowadays, the natural objects used to make colours are difficult to acquire. Moreover, extraction of colours from the natural substances is a very painstaking and time-consuming process. Although his principal occupation is mask making and making of gates, sculptures, and decoration of the Vaishnavite worshipping centres, today he uses only the colours available in the markets. He knows how to extract different colours from various natural objects but never uses these colours to his creation.

Sri Dharmakanta Goswami, aged 73 years, eldest son of renowned mask maker *satradhikar* late Rudrakanta Deva Goswami, is a physically challenged person. He is partially deaf and dumb, and his sole occupation is making of mask, bust, and other decorative objects integral to the culture of the *satras*. He received artist pension of the Government of Assam in the year 2007. He made a good number of masks and other decorative objects, some of which are purchased by the devotees and tourists, including the foreigners. In the year 2007 he made a beautiful mask of the monkey king Sugriva. It is pertinent to note here that Sugriva is one of the important characters of the epic *Ramayana*.

To make those masks at first he had selected a bamboo, locally known as *jati banh*, which was not immature or very mature. He cut the bamboo horizontally into a few pieces with the help of a sharp machete. Then these pieces were immersed in a natural water source (*doba*) situated in front of their house by the side of the principal village path. After seven days, he took out the bamboo tubes and dried them in sunshine. Then he selected one tube and vertically divided it into eleven pieces with the help of the machete. From two bamboo pieces he prepared many thin splits, and then wove them in open hexagonal pattern to prepare the base of the mask. The open periphery of this structure was tied to a more or less oval ring of bamboo split.

Sri Goswami took two pieces of old cotton cloth of about 12 inches by 14 inches in size. He prepared a paste of *kumarmati* and water. He wiped this paste on both sides of cotton cloths and covered the upper side of the basket. In the same manner he added the paste into the second piece of cloth and put it over the uncovered portion of woven base. Then he kept the structure for drying in the sunshine in his courtyard. The next day, he again made a paste of *Kumarmati*, cow-dung, and water, and added it to the front side of the mask to provide the initial shape of the monkey king. Then he dried it in sunshine for two days. At first he covered the mask with a thin layer of the paste and then he re-applied the paste all over the surface of the mask to give it the shape of the monkey king as described in the scripture. Again, he dried it in sunshine for two days. Before completely drying it, some cracks were seen to develop over the mask. The surface of the mask was then scrapped by a bamboo scraper, and then covered with a thin fluid prepared by adding cow-dung and *kumar mati* in water. Drying and covering crazes by the fluid was repeated for five days and finally he coloured the mask. After colouring, embellishment was done and long brown hair, a beautiful crown, and eye-catching ear ornaments were added to the mask. It should be noted here that it is a facial mask (*mukh mukha*) and to complete it, he took eleven days.

Sri Koshakanta Deva Goswami (78 years old), the present *satradhikar* of Natun Chamaguri Satra, is a stalwart mask maker. All his four sons (one recently died of jaundice) are initiated to mask making. He has two grandsons, Rupam (14 years) and Anupam (11 years); they are students of Class IX and Class IV in the high school, respectively, situated within the village. Rupam and Anupam also make masks and some of the masks made by Rupam were bought by foreign tourists. From his childhood, Sri Deva Goswami learnt the art of mask making from the senior mask makers of the Natun Chamaguri Satra through the process of socialization. In the past he used natural colours to paint his creations. However, at present he uses colours available in the market. Sri Deva Goswami is of the opinion that though it is difficult to obtain colours from different natural objects, these colours are eye catching and remain as it is for a long period. The colours, particularly yellow and violet, bought from the market fade up within a short period. Even today he desires to paint his masks with natural colours, but due to old age he is unable to prepare natural colours through the strenuous process. Moreover, the ingredients for making natural colours are not easily available within the village or in its vicinity.

4.3 TYPE OF MASKS

There are three types of masks at Majuli. These are: *mukh mukha, cho mukha*, and *lotokai mukha. Mukh mukha* is worn over the face. *Cho mukha* is very big in size and covers almost the whole body of a person. Sometimes, a *cho mukha* is made 2 to 3.5 metres in height above the waist of the wearer. The huge structure of such a mask reveals the aura of the character portrayed. It is pertinent to note here that in comparison to the huge structure of such a mask, they are very light due to the raw materials used and the intricate manner of mask making. Due to its huge structure, a *cho mukha* is generally tied to the body of the wearer from inside with ropes. *Lotokai mukha* is akin to *cho mukha* except its small size. Due to its small size, the wearer can easily control it and, therefore, *lotokai mukha* is not tied to the body of the wearer. *Lotokai mukha* is also known as *lotokari mukha*. A *cho mukha,* sometimes a *lotokai mukha,* also is a combination of a few easily separable parts.

Anandiram Bora, aged 65 years, is a resident of Natun Chamaguri Village of Majuli. He is a petty businessman, and generally takes part in ritualistic plays occasionally organized in the *satra*. A number of times he performed the role of Ravana, Narasimha, etc. To perform such roles, he has to wear *cho mukha* and *lotokai mukha*. In comparision to the size of the mask, he has a small physique. However, he informed that it is not a difficult task to act wearing medium or big size masks because they are very light in comparison to their size. He also said that sometimes the head of the mask remains above his head and, therefore, for the easy movement in portraying the role of such characters two holes are made in some part of the body of the mask through which he can see easily. When he has to wear the mask of the demon-king Ravana, he has to wear four pieces of the mask—the ten heads, twenty hands, ten in right side and ten in the left, and the body to the waist. The lower part of the body is covered by integral costumes. In the village, after performing a particular role in a ritualistic play many people address him by the name of the character as Ravana or Kumbhakarna.

Sri Rupam Goswami, aged 14 years, grandson of the *satradhikar* Sri Koshakanta Deva Goswami of Natun Chamaguri Satra is a student of Class IX of the local high school. He performed the role of Krishna in many ritualistic plays of the *satra*. It is pertinent to note here that Lord Vishnu is the principal god of the Vaishnavas. They also worship Lord Krishna because Krishna is the full incarnation of Lord Vishnu. Sri Rupam Goswami has to perform the role of Krishna by undergoing fasting and observing many taboos. To perform the role of Lord Krishna, wearing of mask is not required. As Lord Krishna appeared as a human being to eradicate the evils from the earth, he has to kill a good number of demons and demonesses. All these demons and demonesses have to wear masks. In most of the *bhaonas,* Sri Rupam has to kill different demons as Lord Krishna.

It should be noted here that traditionally female roles are played by the males in the ritualistic plays of a *satra*. In performing the roles of the gods, goddesses, and human beings, generally masks are not worn. However, the life of Lord Krishna is full of many incidents where he has to kill a good number of ferocious demons and demonesses. To depict the characters of these demons and demonesses, all the actors have to wear integral masks. In the context of a *satra,* besides in *ankia bhaona* (Vaishnavite one-act play), masks are also worn in *Rasotsava* (frolic of Lord Krishna) with the *gopis* (consorts). There are a good number of *ankia bhaonas* written by the Vaishnavite saints of Assam, and also by the *satradhikars* and other devotees. All these plays centred round Lord Krishna and have depicted the heroic activities of the God. In such plays many characters of demons and demonesses are knitted and in a *bhaona* these characters have to wear masks. In the autumn season, it is described in the Hindu scriptures, Lord Krishna involved in merry-making with the *gopis* on *purnima* (full moon night) of the month of *Kati* (October-November). In Natun Chamaguri Satra, the *Keli Gopala* play is performed every year on this occasion. In this drama it is depicted that when Lord Krishna was dancing with the *gopis* in a dense forest known as Vrindavana, some of the demons attacked the *gopis* and Lord Krishna rescued them from the grip of the demons with his intelligence and vigour. In the Natun Chamaguri Satra, among the festivals that are observed according to the Indian calendar, mention may be made of Guru Kirtana (prayer held at the anniversaries of the Vaishnava Gurus), Phalgotsava (festival of colour), Palnama (a kind of continuous prayer), Janmastami (birth ritual of Lord Krishna), Pachati (name-giving ceremony of Lord Krishna on the fifth day of his birth), etc. Generally, the *bhaonas* are held in Rasotsava, Palnama, etc. Before such festivals generally the new masks are made, and the old masks are repaired and re-painted.

The festivals of the *satra* are performed with pomp and gaiety. These create a socio-religious wave throughout the village. The kith and kins, friends and well-wishers from far and near come to the Natun Chamaguri village and reside at different households. During these periods, the village vibrates with the sound of *khol* (Vaishnavite drum), cymbals, and other Vaishnavite instruments, and the melodious tunes of prayers. Each household of the village seems to be gripped in a religious fervour, and the whole village is covered by the fragrance of the incense sticks and incense powder. *Bhaona* is the main attraction of many Vaishnavite festivals observed at the Natun Chamaguri Satra. People from all walks of life and from all age groups enjoy *bhaonas* in the *satra.* The following cases will give an idea about the attraction of *bhaona* in the Natun Chamaguri Satra.

Miss Jonmani, aged 14 years, is a student of Class IX of Marigaon Higher Secondary School of Marigaon District, Assam. Four years back, her elder sister was married to a youth of Natun Chamaguri village. She came with the new bride from Marigaon to Natun Chamaguri just after her sister's marriage. She found that journey very tedious one because to reach Majuli everyone has to cross the vast Brahmaputra River. After a few months of her elder sister's marriage, Jonmani was invited by the husband of her elder sister to Natun Chamaguri along with her family members on the occasion of Rasotsava. Initially, she was reluctant to visit Natun Chamaguri remembering the troublesome memory of crossing the mighty Brahmaputra in a ferry boat, which generally takes 1 hour 30 minutes to two hours. On the persuasion of her mother, she went to Natun Chamaguri along with her father and younger brother. In that visit she got the chance to see the *bhaona* entitled *Keli-Gopala* in the Natun Chamaguri Satra. Miss Jonmoni was spellbound by watching the performance of the *bhaona,* and from that time she went to her elder sister's house every year to enjoy the *bhaona* in Rasotsava.

Sri Rajat Chandra Bharali, aged 55 years, a permanent resident of Guwahati city of Assam, is an orthodox devotee of the Vaishnavite cult. He is a petty businessman and desires to attend all the ritual observances of the *satras* of Majuli. However, it is not possible for him to attend all those festivals of Majuli. When he can manage his time, he usually visits Majuli at least to pay his respect to the *satras.* According to Sri Bharali, there are four *satras* in Assam, viz., Auniati, Dakshinpat, Garmur, and Kuruabahi, which are treated as the supreme Vaishnavite *satras.* Among these four *satras,* Auniati, Dakshinpat, and Garmur are situated at Majuli, which provide a special status in the Vaishnavite environ to the large riverine island. Srimanta Sankaradeva had established the first *satra* at Majuli; for such reasons this island is treated as the epitome of Assam's Vaishnavite culture. These factors attracted Sri Bharali immensely and he used to visit it when he could manage his time. Generally, he desires to visit Majuli at least during the observance of Rasotsava. He opines that because he is not much educated, therefore, it is difficult for him to go through the Vaishnavite scriptures, most of which are written as poems, and to acquire the meaning of those poems. In Rasotsava, when he observes the *bhaonas,* generally at the Natun Chamaguri Satra, he feels that good always wins over evils. According to him, in a *bhaona* one can easily identify the 'good' and 'evil'. Lord Krishna is the epitome of goodness and the evils are generally projected through shrewd and ferocious looking masks worn by the actors who perform the roles of the demons and demonesses. By observing different *bhaonas,* now he knows the underlying meaning of many Vaishnavite scriptures.

'The identification of specific emotions and their facial expression has been, and still is, the object of intense scientific scrutiny' (Bouissac, 2001: 75). Every society has some sanctions and strictures regarding the facial expressions of its members. In Assamese society also, there are pristine norms and values to regulate the facial muscles in the different social contexts. The facial expression, which is not accepted in a society, is also depicted through the masks. 'The mask does not depict a single emotion at a particular time, it is not a portrait of who fears, who fights, who dies; it is symbol of fear, war, death' (Monte, 1969: 9). Along with the ferocious looking masks of different demons and deities of the Chamaguri and the Natun Chamaguri Satra, there are a few masks which render very calm and quiet appearances. The masks of mighty Ravana, Garuda (the mount of Vishnu), etc. emit notable peace, coyness, and amiability. Due to the submissiveness, the main pulse of Vaishnavism, many powerful characters of Hindu scriptures are also depicted through calm and quiet looking masks.

4.4 MASK AND GENDER

Mask making is a male job; however, the females are also not tabooed from making it. It is not a common skill and is practiced by only a few male members of the families integrally related to the *satra* management. The art of mask making and often their forms and functions are passed down through lineages (*bamsa*) or families (*pariyal*). Mask making is not taught, but learnt by the interested juniors from the seniors through the process of socialization. The skill is indispensably related to the *satra* organization, and no person outside a *satra* is known for making it, though there is no restriction in such pursuit. However, at present some of the youths of the Natun Chamaguri Satra have initiated to this skill through an organization known as Sukumar Kalapeeth established by the expert mask maker Sri Hem Chandra Goswami.

The Natun Chamaguri Satra is resourced with the art of famous mask making since its inception. The tradition of mask making of the *satra* is carried out from the Prachin Chamaguri Satra wherefrom it is bifurcated. The spellbounding ability in mask making of the forefathers of *satradhikars* of the Natun Chamaguri Satra like Tankeswara Deva Goswami, Moksheswara Deva, Raseswara Deva, Chaitanya Deva, Saisava Chandra Deva Goswami, etc. are still remembered. Till today, some of the creations of those stalwarts are seen in the Prachin Chamaguri Satra. In the Natun Chamaguri Satra also, there are many stalwarts like Kamal Chandra Deva Goswami (*satradhikar)*, Bhimakanta Deva (*deka satradhikar*), Bansidhar Deva Goswami, etc. who have remarkable reputation for their creations of beautiful masks. The Chamaguri Satra has a thought-provoking history of 236 years, and from that *satra*, the art of mask making is spread to different places. The present *satradhikar* of Natun Chamaguri Satra Sri Koshakanta Deva Goswami, Sri Umakanta Deva Goswami, Sri Phanidhar Goswami, *deka satradhikar* of Prachin Chamaguri Satra, and Jaychandra Goswami of the same *satra*, are some of the reputed persons whose names should be mentioned for their untiring devotion to add the eye-catching value in mask making.

Late *satradhikar* Rudrakanta Dev Goswami was a praiseworthy mask maker who added new aesthetic dimensions to the tradition of mask making. He was honoured with the artist pension in 1988 by the Government of Assam. All his three sons, Dharmakanta, Hem Chandra, and Krishnakanta, are stalwart mask makers. Now Krishnakanta works as a lecturer of sculpture in the Government Art College of Assam. Hemchandra trained many groups of youth in and outside the state the mask making style of Assam. In 1980, Hemchandra established an institute, viz., Sukumar Kalapeeth, in the Chamaguri Village, to train the village youths the art of mask making. The beautiful mask of the demon-king Ravana made by the Late *satradhikar* Umakanta Dev Goswami is preserved in the State Museum of Assam. The present *satradhikar*, Koshakanta Dev Goswami and his son Prasanna are also mask makers of repute. Sri Koshakanta Deva Goswami made some figures of birds from the barks of areca nut in 1981-1982 in the competition arranged by the NCERT, Assam Branch, and has received the National Award. Sri Koshakanta Deva Goswami was honoured with artist pension by the Government of Assam in 1997. In the year 2003, he was awarded the Sangeet Nataka Academy Award by the Government of India.

> In the simplest societies every individual can and does perform all the secular activities of his community, except so far as there may be

> artificial restraints of his so doing, and as a rule he can make any of the implements he requires, but, even so, there are usually to be found men who are more expert than others. Thus in some societies this expertness gives rise to special craftsmen; or certain men may in their spare time specialize in certain crafts. Where special craftsmen are found, it is necessary to make inquiries as to their status and how they are paid. Iron workers in Africa may form a despised or Pariah class or they may have special privileges and position. Canoe-builders, or other carpenters, may have a high social status. The craftsmen should be considered from economic, magical, religious, legendary and mythological points of view (A Committee of the Royal Anthropological Institute of Great Britain and Ireland, 1954: 222-223).

Although anyone can make a mask, there are only a few persons in Majuli who are devoted to this skill of art. Among those mask makers, some have shown rare ability in creation of masks. It has been already stated that Alengi Narasimha Satra and Bihimpur Satra also a praiseworthy reputation for mask making. The late *satradhikars* Lilakanta Mahanta and Priya Kanta Mahanta of Alengi Narasimha Satra were well known for their artistic abilities of mask making. Both the sons of late Lilakanta Mahanta, i.e., Sri Lalit Mahanta and Sri Golap Mahanta, are mask makers of repute. Sri Krishna Mahanta and Sri Deven Mahanta of Bihimpur Satra are also notable mask makers. Some of the residential devotees of Natun Kamalabari Satra have acquired the ability of mask making and use to prepare different masks according to the needs of the *satra.*

Sri Hemchandra Goswami, aged 53 years, is a reputed mask maker of the Natun Chamaguri Satra. He had created a good number of masks following the traditional process of mask making, learned through socialization, principally from his *satradhikar* father late Rudrakanta Deva Goswami. Although he followed the traditional method of mask making, he added some conspicuous dimensions for the improvement of this art without destroying the pristine values. It is indispensable to add a paste of cow-dung, *kumar mati,* and water to give the shape of a mask. Sri Goswami used to add a small quantity of kerosene to this paste. He opines that adding of kerosene gives the mask a longer life because easily available kerosene acts as an insecticide. He also made some of the masks with movable parts, which provide more effectiveness to the mask. He made the ornaments to the head, horn, etc. of the masks in such a manner that the ornaments moved freely adding attractiveness to his creations. To make the masks lighter-nowadays he adds more thermocol instead of adding more paste of *kumarmati*, etc. to a mask. Adding of thermocol makes the mask lighter and the actors feel comfortable by wearing these masks. Besides the traditional masks he also makes small masks for the decoration of drawing room, motor car, etc. He made a good number of concrete statues in different places of the state.

4.5 SOME ASPECTS INTEGRAL TO MASKS

It has been already described that a mask has different uses like social, religious, funerary, commemorative, therapeutic, theatrical, festive, etc. However, in Majuli masks are mostly used in theatrical performances in different rituals and festivals of the *satra*. There are only a few *satras* in Assam where the tradition of mask making is prevalent. From the mask making, *satras* masks are taken to the other *satras* on loan or as donation because masks are integral to the *satra* culture and most of the rituals and festivals where religious plays should be performed are not possible without masks. Generally, each mask displays two feelings—good and evil. There are a good number of incidents which happened for not obeying the traditional strictures in mask making. At Biswanath Chariali, a culture centre of Assam, situated in the Sonitpur district, *Bare Saharia Bhaona* (Vaishnavite plays of a good number of villages) is held annually. In that festival at least twelve *bhaonas* are performed simultaneously by the people of different localities where thousands of spectators thronged. Different masks are made by the makers strictly obeying the description of scriptures and tradition of the locality. Therefore, the Narasimha of Majuli resembles more a horse than a lion. Once an enthusiastic mask maker made a huge mask of Kalinaga, the wicked serpent king, defying the traditional pattern by increasing the number of heads in the mask. When Lord Krishna started dancing over the head of the Kalinaga, the furious serpent king left the stage and moved towards a nearby big tank along with Lord Krishna. A havoc was created among the actors and spectators, and only after an earnest prayer to the Almighty, Kalinaga stopped and fainted.

Before the performances in a *bhaona*, the actors have to go through some rigid taboos, and the people believe if someone does not maintain the taboos, some accidents may occur in the *bhaona*. During the recent past, a *bhaona* was performed in the Natun Chamaguri Satra where a handsome teenager acted as Lord Krishna. During the *bhaona* he came to a frenzy and started moving to a nearby pool leaving the stage of the *bhaona*. The village elders somehow managed to stop him after which the boy fainted immediately.

There are a good number of superstitions associated with masks.

> What is more interesting is that these (masks) are considered to be living. This is evident from the using of *chaki* (lamp) at night in front of the masks. There is a common belief that these rival masks may start quarreling if these are kept in the dark........ Why do such beliefs continue? The people not related to rural cultural setting where these masks are used may take it as a matter of superstition, but it is a reality in the rural area where the boundary between the past and the present is a diffused one (Roy; 1985: 59-60).

In the Natun Chamaguri Satra, some of the masks like the mask of Narasimha, Ravana, etc. are respected much more than the others. After the performance in a *bhaona,* these are kept in a clean place and earthen lamps are lit and incense sticks are burnt every dusk in front of these. The worn-out masks of Narasimha, Ravana, etc. are immersed respectfully in the nearby river by playing Vaishnavite drum, cymbals, etc. by a group of devotees chanting prayers.

Levi-Strauss (1977: 263-64) writes:

> ...... spilt representation as a trait common to mask cultures. ... Not all mask cultures employ spilt representation. We do not find it (at least in as developed a form) in the art of the Pueblo of the American Southwest nor in that of New Guinea. In both these cultures, however, masks play a considerable role. Masks also represent ancestors, and by wearing the mask the actor incarnates the ancestor. What, therefore, is the difference? The difference is that, in contrast to the civilizations we have considering here, there is no chain of privileges, emblems, and degrees of prestige which, by means of masks, validate social hierarchy through the primacy of genealogies. The supernatural does not have as its chief function the creation of castes and classes. The world of masks constitutes a pantheon rather than an ancestrality. Thus, the actor incarnates the god only on the intermittent occasions of feasts and ceremonies. He does not acquire from the god, by a continuous process of creation at each moment of social life, his titles, his rank, his position in the status hierarchy. The parallelism which we established is thus confirmed, rather than invalidated, by these examples. The mutual independence of the plastic and graphic components corresponds to the more flexible interplay between the social and supernatural orders, in the same way that split representation expresses

> the strict conformity of the actor to his role and of social rank to myths, ritual, and pedigrees. This conformity is so vigorous that, in order for the individual to be dissociated from his social role, he must be torn asunder.

In the context of Natun Chamaguri Satra, the masks do not represent the deceased forefathers or a medium to communicate them. These masks do not determine the rank or status of the persons who wear them. In that *satra,* masks are generally worn at the ritualistic plays, and during that time the actors become the mythological characters, and the spectators also pay respect or regard to these characters forgetting their actual identity and accepting them as the characters they performed in the play.

In the Natun Chamaguri village, where the study *satra* is situated, most of the persons practised mask making as a primary occupation. All the mask makers belong to Kayastha caste, though the traditional occupation of the Kayastha is scribing. In the *Census of India*, Vol. III, Assam (1931: 211), it is written, 'Caste in the Assam valley is not, as elsewhere, chiefly a functional division, it is really a racial division and functional caste are very few' (cited in Cantlie, 1984: 7). There is no caste in Assam, the members of which practise mask making as the traditional occupation. Like a mask maker, an idol (*murti*) maker is also referred to as *khanikar* by the Assamese people. The idol making is also not practised by any Assamese caste as their traditional occupation. However, there are some people in Assam who have used the term *khanikar* as their surname. In old days, their forefathers expertised in making different sculptures, principally from wood and clay. A mask maker is respected by the people for his ability. Till the recent past, a mask maker did not receive any remuneration for his creation except for honour and prestige. His creations were taken by the people to perform religious theatrical performances without giving him any money. Now a mask maker earns nominal money for his skill; however, it is not sufficient to maintain his livelihood and, therefore, he has to earn money doing other jobs to maintain his livelihood, and to satisfy his aesthetic urge, he makes masks.

5

Available Masks of Natun Chamaguri Satra

Natun Chamaguri Satra has a praiseworthy history of mask making. It has been already mentioned that the mask makers of the *satra* made three types of masks—*mukh mukha, cho mukha, lotokai* or *lotokari mukha.* In the absence of a proper method of preservation, most of the old masks are found in a dilapidated condition, especially the body, arms, etc. of the *cho* and *lotokai mukha* are found damaged by insects and weather. Besides these masks made for fulfilling the need of theatrical performances, both ritualistic and modern, the mask makers of the *satra* occasionally shaped some animal figures, which could not actually be categorized under the heading of mask. The found animal figures are very few in number, and handled by men instead of being worn by performers. The available masks of the *satra* are described below in alphabetical sequences:

Sl. no	:	1
Plate no	:	29
Name of the mask	:	Aghasura
English equivalent	:	Agha, the demon
Type	:	*Cho mukha* (only facial part is shown in the plate)

Mask maker	:	Sri Dharmakanta Goswami (74 yrs.)
Year of making	:	2000
Condition	:	Good
Maximum height	:	56 cm

Colour

Light violet with straw colour shade to make the scales of the serpent; inner part of the mouth is reddish. Eyeballs are black in while circles; two long fangs are ivory white.

Mythology

Aghasura (*agha* means sin, *asura* means demon), a tricky and ferocious demon, was one of the generals of Kamsa. Kamsa, the maternal uncle of Lord Krishna, was the tyrannical king of Mathura. After the marriage of Kamsa's sister Devaki, it was announced through an *akashvani* (voice from the sky) that Kamsa would be killed by the eighth son of Devaki. He put his sister and her husband Vasudeva in the prison and killed their seven sons; but he failed to kill the eighth, who was Lord Krishna, the human incarnation of Lord Vishnu. Krishna was carried to the house of Nanda, the king of Braja, by the gods. Kamsa tried his best to kill Krishna to get rid of the curse. He sent many wicked demons and demonesses to kill child Krishna. Kamsa sent Aghasura also to kill Krishna. Aghasura assumed the form of a large serpent and Krishna's companions, the cowherds, entered its mouth, mistaking it for a mountain cavern; but Krishna rescued them and killed the demon.

Description

The plate 29 exhibits only the head part of the serpent demon Aghasura. It looks like the head of a huge live python. The remaining part of the demon (not shown in the plate) also looks like that of a python. The whole body is covered with meticulously made rough rectangular scales. This mask has a very big mouth, which possesses two long and sharp fangs at the upper jaw. The black eyeballs are encircled by thick white lines. From the head, the body of the mask is gradually tapered towards the end of the tail.

Sl. no	:	2
Plate no	:	30
Name of the mask	:	Anantanaga
English equivalent	:	Eternal (*ananta*) serpent (*naga*)
Type	:	*Cho mukha*

Mask maker	:	Sri Prasanna Goswami (40 years)
Year of making	:	1998
Condition	:	Slightly distort
Maximum height	:	2 mt

Colour

In this mask, an eye-catching combination of white, pink, and brown colour is noticeable except in the top of the heads, which is milk white. The body, head tops, five hoods, and the Y-shaped tongues are in pink colour. Inner side of the *fanas* (expansion of the head), and the hoods of the serpent are adorned with intricate diamond-shaped designs of brown colour. The body and the vertically middle line of the hoods are coloured in pink in such a way that that it seems as if a number of bangles are kept one over another.

Mythology

Ananta naga possesses one thousand hoods (only five in the mask as per tradition). It is a revered serpent whose status is more or less equal to the heavenly bodies as he is allowed to spread his hoods over the body of Lord Vishnu, the protector of the universe. When Lord Vishnu was in eternal sleep (*ananta sayana*) over the *Kshirod sagara* (sea of milk), on the bed made by Ananta naga by coiling his enormously elongated body, and also protected him from sunshine and rain by spreading his hoods. It is pertinent to note that one of the names of Lord Vishnu is also Ananta.

Description

It is a very big mask of gigantic mythological serpent Ananta naga with five (representing a thousand) heads. The adjoining body part of the head (around 1 mt) is cylindrical and more or less perpendicular. Rear part of the body is broader than that of the front part (in plate, only the head part of the serpent is shown). The five heads are joined to form more or less half a circle, the upper periphery of which possesses five apexes to indicate the five heads of the mighty serpent. Each of the heads possesses a single Y-shaped prominent tongue.

Sl.no.	:	3
Plate no.	:	31
Name of the mask	:	Bagh
English equivalent	:	Tiger
Type	:	*Mukh mukha*

Mask maker	:	Sri Koshakanta Deva Goswami (78 years)
Year of making	:	2002
Condition	:	Excellent
Maximum height	:	34 cm

Colour

Colours are artistically applied to make the mask look like a real leopard.

Description

It is a beautiful mask with a reddish nose and open mouth; a few teeth on the upper jaw and two teeth on lower jaw are conspicuous. The two teeth in the lower jaw are sharp and bigger than those of the upper jaw. The tongue is visible, and it is of pink colour with blue spots. Eyes are lively and a few long hair are present on both sides of the face below the nose. All over the head, beautiful spots like that of the real leopard are there.

Sl no.	:	4
Plate no.	:	32
Local name	:	Bakasura
English equivalent	:	Baka (literally stork), the demon
Type	:	*Cho mukha*
Mask maker	:	Sri Hem Chandra Goswami (53 years)
Year of making	:	2005
Condition	:	Good
Maximum length	:	3 mt

Colour

The base colour of the mask is white; the beak is yellow, inner side of which is red; eyes are black encircled by red lines.

Mythology

Bakasura was a ferocious demon and the subordinate of Kamsa. He was sent by the demon-king Kamsa, who is also the maternal uncle of Krishna, to kill child Krishna. When child Krishna along with his brother Balarama were playing on the bank of the river Yamuna at Gokula, Bakasura appeared before them in the form of a terrible looking huge stork. He opened his ferocious beak and swallowed Krishna. The touch of Krishna burnt the throat of the bird and ultimately he died vomiting Krishna alive.

Description

The mask of Bakasura looks like a huge stork. It has a large and long beak, which is widely opened. Eyes are very small and circular in shape.

The neck is long, cylindrical, and slender. It has two wings on both sides of the body, which are movable. The tail of the bird is short.

Sl. no.	:	5
Plate no.	:	33
Local name	:	Bali
English equivalent	:	Bali, the monkey king
Type	:	*Mukh mukha*
Mask maker	:	Sri Hem Chandra Goswami (53 years)
Year of making	:	2006
Condition	:	Very good
Maximum height	:	43 cm

Colour

The base colour of the mask is pinkish brown; eyebrows, eyeballs, and eyelashes are black in colour; hair on the head and face are golden brown; tip of the nose and lips are pink. On the forehead of the mask two elongated horizontal and vertical lines are present, one overlapping the other drawn with white, maroon, and yellow colour. The crown on the head is beautifully decorated with white, red, golden, and yellow, and the two rings of the ears are in pink, yellow, and black colour.

Mythology

Bali was a pious and mighty monkey king of Kiskindhya. He was brave and powerful. Once Bali received a boon that he would get half the strength of the foe who faced him, and for that it is not possible for anyone to defeat him in direct combat. After Sita had been abducted by Ravana, Rama and Lakshmana wandered about in the forest and they met Hanumana, a pious monkey, who took them to his king Sugriva. Sri Rama and Sugriva entered into a treaty, by which Rama was to kill Bali, the elder brother of Sugriva, and reinstate Sugriva as the king of Kishkindhya. For that Sugriva had to assist Rama in his war against Ravana to rescue Sita. After the agreement Sugriva fought with Bali. Rama put a flower garland around the neck of Sugriva to identify him from Bali because both the brothers looked very much alike. When Bali and Sugriva were fighting, Rama instantly sent an arrow toward the breast of Bali when he was looking sideways. The reason being it was not possible to kill Bali directly for the boon granted to him. So, ultimately, Bali was killed by Rama, and Sugriva reinstated the king of Kiskindhya. Bali was supposed to be the son of Indra and believed to be born from his mother's hair (*bala*), hence the name Bali. Tara was his wife, and he had a son called Angada.

Description

The mask of Bali is a very impressive one. Due to its marked prognathism in facial portion, it looks like a typical monkey. The eyes are big and prominent; eyebrows are arch-shaped and in between the two eyebrows in the forehead, one beautiful spot is seen; beautifully designed ear-rings are circular in shape; hair on the head and face are long and golden brown in colour; nose is short. The crown on the head is meticulously designed; on the base of it, one red colour strip is drawn with a good number of white lines. Just above this strip in the middle portion of the crown, one flame-like structure is present coloured in red, black, white, and golden yellow. On the top of the crown, more or less triangle-shaped structure in silver and red colour is seen and its back side is encircled by a circular shaped-plate with floral designs.

Sl. no.	:	6
Plate no.	:	34
Local name	:	Baraha (I)
English equivalent	:	The boar (an incarnation of Lord Vishnu)
Type	:	*Mukh mukha*
Mask maker	:	Sri Hem Chandra Goswami (53 years)
Year of making	:	1999
Condition	:	Slightly distored
Maximum height	:	56 cm

Colour

Base is light blue, eyes look like that of human; a U-shaped white with a decorative spot on forehead is there between the eyes. The crown in the head is of golden and white colour. Hair are golden; two white big lunar-shaped teeth are prominent.

Mythology

Baraha is the seventh incarnation of Lord Vishnu. He took this incarnation to save Mother Earth (*Basundhara*). Once upon a time, Basundhara was infested by a good number of notorious demons who made the earth full of troubles and problems. The sages and the devoted people were scared and troubled by these demons. Due to the malevolent activities of these demons, Mother Earth lost her original position and gradually pushed downward. Basundhara's heart was full of agony and sorrow, and she propitiated Lord Vishnu to save her dignity and entity. Then Lord Vishnu took the form of a huge *Baraha* and with his two long and strong teeth killed the demons and placed Basundhara in proper position.

Description

This facial mask resembles more to a human being than to a boar. The mask is beautifully decorated with two obliquely placed human eyes; the ears resemble horse ears instead of boar's; the mask possesses golden hair; a beautiful crown meticulously decorated with golden and white colours is seen over the forehead.

Sl. no.	:	7
Plate no.	:	35
Local name	:	Baraha (II)
English equivalent	:	The boar (an incarnation of Lord Vishnu)
Type	:	*Lotokai mukha*
Mask maker	:	Sri Hem Chandra Goswami (53 years)
Year of making	:	2001
Condition	:	Good
Maximum height	:	130 cm

Colour

Base of the mask is dull white, eyes are yellowish with reddish tinge under prominent black eyebrows. Hooves are black.

Mythology

Same as Sl. No. 6

Description

It is a full mask of *Lotokai* type, which looks like a real boar except the legs. Because the mask has to be worn by an actor, the front legs are made longer than that of the actual boar. There is a big circular hole at the rear part of the stomach of the mask through which the performer inserts the upper part of his body. It should be mentioned here that the performer's legs are carefully covered with costumes to represent the hind limbs of the boar. The mask has two long lunar-shaped teeth. A crown meticulously decorated with golden and white colours is seen over the forehead.

Sl. no.	:	8
Plate no.	:	36
Local name	:	Burha Bamun (I)

English equivalent	:	Old Brahmana
Type	:	*Mukh mukha*
Mask maker	:	Sri Prasanna Goswami (40 years)
Year of the making	:	1990
Condition	:	Good
Maximum height	:	26 cm

Colour

Base colour is blue; lips are red; eyebrows are black; eyeballs are red circled by thick black lines; prominent, golden lotus petal-shaped golden spot on forehead surrounded by red lines.

Description

The mask is beautiful and looks like that of a clown; ears are bigger than that of humans. Nose is flat; lips are twisted in a ludicrous manner.

Sl. no.	:	9
Plate no.	:	37
Local name	:	Burha Bamun (II)
English equivalent	:	Old Brahmana
Type	:	*Mukh mukha*
Mask maker	:	Sri Prasanna Goswami (40 years)
Year of making	:	1990
Condition	:	Good
Maximum height	:	25 cm

Colour

Base colour is golden; lips are red; eyebrows and eyeballs are black; more or less diamond-shaped spot is present on the forehead over which a cream colour circular spot is present.

Description

It is a colourful attractive mask with two prominent big ears. Nose is broad and flat; mouth is broad and lips are pressed in a manner as if to hide some conspiracy.

Sl. no.	:	10
Plate no.	:	38
Local name	:	*Byadha / Jalowa* (I)
English equivalent	:	Hunter / Fisherman
Type	:	*Mukh mukha*
Mask maker	:	Sri Koshakanta Deva Goswami (78 years)

Year of making	:	1994
Condition	:	Very good
Maximum height	:	24 cm

Colour

The mask is meticulously coloured with white, black, red, and pink colours. Both the eyebrows and moustache are black in colour.

Description

The mask is bald-headed, flat-nosed, and bulk-teethed. Thick moustache with a pair of broad eyes provides the mask a funny look. Mouth is very broad and the teeth are conspicuous. Two wavy marks of black colour are present on the chin. Both the mouth and chin are movable according to the will of the wearer. The mask is put on by the hunter or fishermen in ritualistic theatres according to the situation.

Sl. no.	:	11
Plate no.	:	39
Local name	:	*Byadha / Jalowa* (II)
English equivalent	:	Hunter / Fisherman
Type	:	*Mukh mukha*
Mask maker	:	Sri Kosakanta Deva Goswami (78 year)
Year of making	:	1994
Condition	:	Very good
Maximum height	:	25 cm

Colour

The mask is coloured with white, black, grey, and brown colours. The hair, eyebrows, and moustache are grey in colour.

Description

The mask possesses a parrot nose, oblique eyes, and big ears with white circular spot in the earlobe. The mouth and chin of the mask move at the will of the wearer. The mask also has vertical black colour lines on the chin. This mask is put on by the hunter or fisherman in ritualistic theatres according to the situation.

Sl. no.	:	12
Plate no.	:	40
Local name	:	*Chakravata*
English equivalent	:	the demon of cyclone
Type	:	*Mukh mukha*

Pl. 1. Kamakhya temple in Nilachal Hills of Assam.

Pl. 2. Dancing in Rongali Bihu festivals.

Pl. 3. Towards Majuli in boat.

Pl. 4. A peripherial view of Majuli.

Pl. 5. A view of a namghar.

Pl. 6. A view of a satra.

Pl. 7. Entrance of the Natun Chamaguri village.

Pl. 8. A residential unit of Natun Chamaguri village.

Pl. 9. A view of the Natun Chamaguri Satra.

Pl. 10. Inside view of the manikut of Prachin Chamaguri Satra.

Pl. 11. The mighty mythological bird Garuda in a satra.

Pl. 12. Garuda, the vehicle of Lord Vishnu, the Protector of the satra.

Pl. 13. A few implements used for mask making.

Pl. 14. Physically challenged Sri Dharmakanta Goswami busy in mask making.

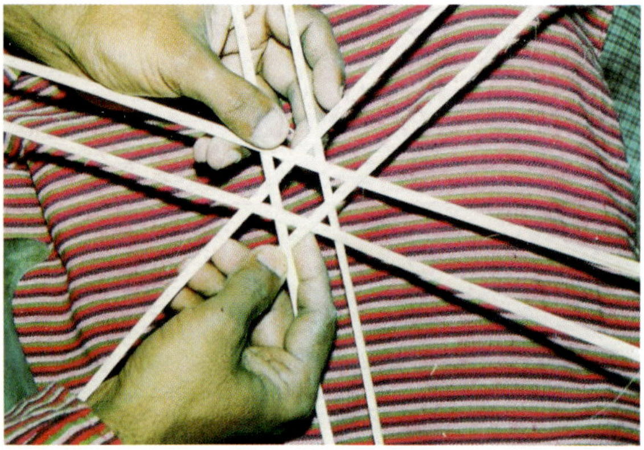

Pl. 15. Open hexagonal pattern used in making the base of a mask.

Pl. 16. Sri Hem Chandra Goswami while making the base of a mask.

Pl. 17. Covering the woven base of a mask with treated cotton fabric.

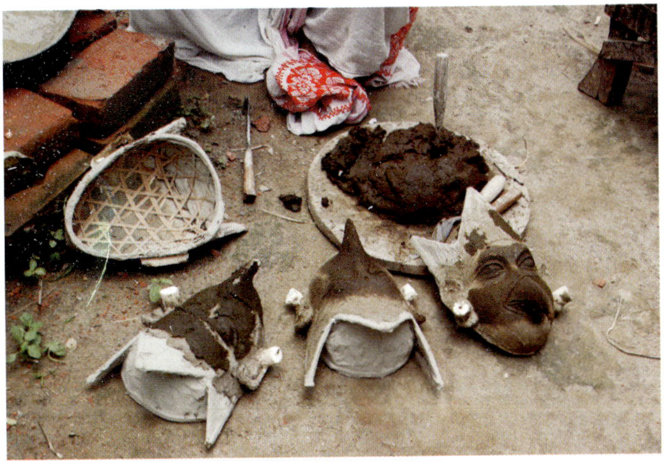

Pl. 18. Bamboo base of masks are plastered with a paste of kumarmati, cowdung, and water.

Pl. 19. Drying the masks.

Pl. 20. Dried-up masks are ready for colouring.

Pl. 21. The satradhikar of Natun Chamaguri Satra while painting a mask.

Pl. 22. Sri Dharmakanta Goswami (l) and Sri Hem Chandra Goswami (r) are busy in mask making.

Pl. 23. Initial prayer before a bhaona.

Pl. 24. A scene from a bhaona.

Pl. 25. An actor as the mythological bird Jatayu in a bhaona.

Pl. 26. A common man transforming him to the demon king Ravana by wearing a mask.

Pl. 27. Playing the role of the monkey king Sugriva in a bhaona.

Pl. 28. A scene from a bhaona.

Pl. 29. The mask of Aghasura.

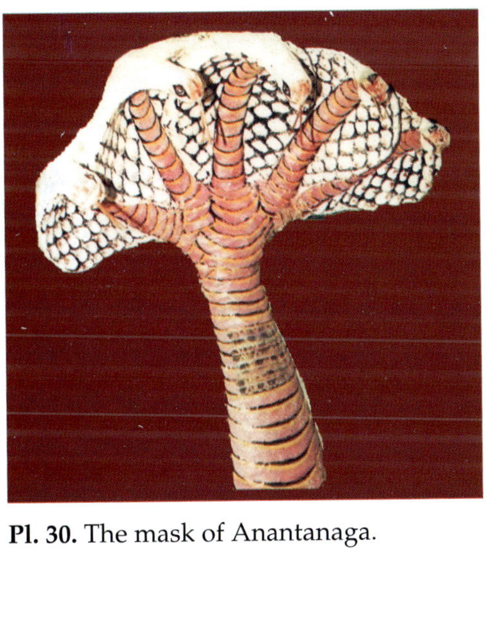

Pl. 30. The mask of Anantanaga.

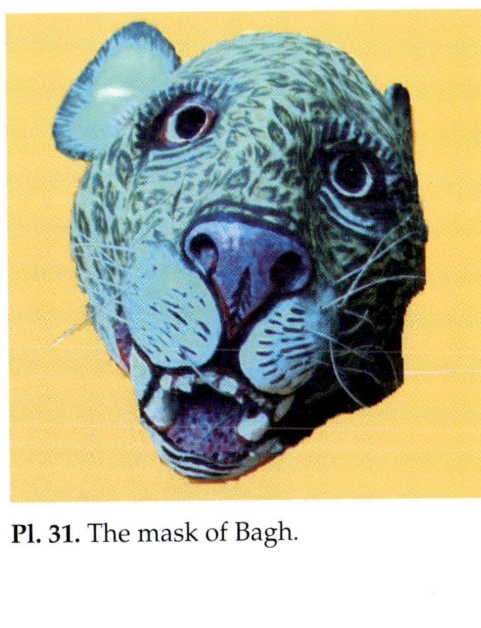

Pl. 31. The mask of Bagh.

Pl. 32. The mask of Bakasura.

Pl. 33. The mask of Bali.

Pl. 34. The mask of Baraha (I).

Pl. 35. The mask of Baraha (II).

Pl. 36. The mask of Burha Bamun (I).

Pl. 37. The mask of Burha Bamun (II).

Pl. 38. The mask of Byadha / Jalowa (I).

Pl. 39. The mask of Byadha / Jalowa (II).

Pl. 40. The mask of Chakravata.

Pl. 41. The mask of Danava (I).

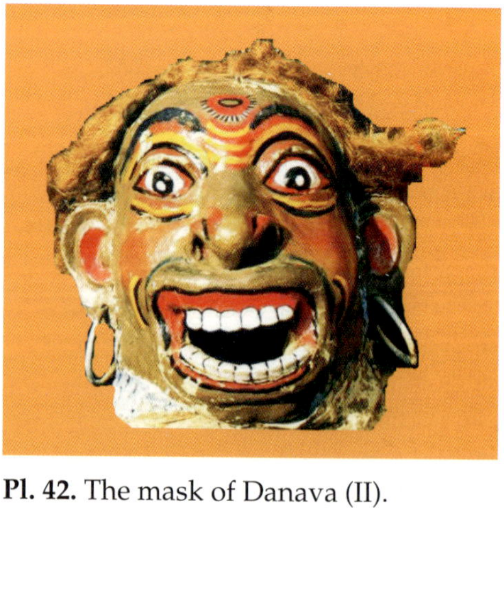

Pl. 42. The mask of Danava (II).

Pl. 43. The mask of Danava (III).

Pl. 44. The mask of Danava (IV).

Pl. 45. The mask of Dhenukasura.

Pl. 46. The mask of Dundubhi.

Pl. 47. The mask of Dushana.

Pl. 48. The mask of Hanumana.

Pl. 49. The mask of Jatayu.

Pl. 50. The mask of Khara.

Pl. 51. The mask of Kumbhakarna.

Pl. 52. The mask of Maricha (I).

Pl. 53. The mask of Maricha (II).

Pl. 54. The mask of Mayavi.

Pl. 55. The mask of Narasimha (I).

Pl. 56. The mask of Narasimha (II).

Pl. 57. The mask of Nila.

Pl. 58. The mask of Pralambasura.

Pl. 60. The mask of Ravana (II).

Pl. 59. The mask of Ravana (I).

Pl. 61. The mask of Ravana (III).

Pl. 62. The mask of Ravana (as beggar).

Pl. 63. The mask of Sankhachura.

Pl. 64. The mask of Simgha.

Pl. 65. The mask of Sugriva.

Pl. 66. The mask of Surpanakha.

Pl. 67. The mask of Taraka.

Pl. 68. The mask of Tarakasura.

Pl. 69. The mask of Trisira.

Mask maker	:	Sri Koshakanta Deva Goswami (78 years)
Year of making	:	1996
Condition	:	Very good
Maximum height	:	46 cm

Colour

The base colour is chocolate brown; lips are very broad and are pink in colour; eyebrows are black. Some wavy black and yellow colour lines are there above the eyebrows. A black colour circular spot is present on the forehead. Semi-circular black and white lines are present at the base of the nose.

Mythology

Chakravata is an aerial demon who is the authority of cyclone. Obeying Kamsa's order, once he snatched baby Krishna and flew to the sky. Though Lord Krishna was a child at that time; he had enormous courage and strength, because he was the full incarnation of Lord Vishnu, and took birth on earth to destroy the evil forces. He killed the demon by squeezing his neck and fell back on earth without a single scar in his body sitting on the breast of the demon.

Description

The mask of Chakravata is meticulously made with a hair knot over the head closely resembling an ant hill. The ears resemble those of an elephant; nose is very flat; eyes express cruelty; face bulges out showing the irregular teeth of upper jaw. Principally black, red, and white colours are used to paint the mask, which provide it a cunning and cruel look.

Sl. no.	:	13
Plate no.	:	41
Local name	:	*Danava / Rakshasha / Daitya* (I)
English equivalent	:	Demon
Type	:	*Mukh mukha*
Mask maker	:	Sri Koshakanta Deva Goswami (78 years)
Year of making	:	1997
Condition	:	Good
Maximum height	:	44 cm

Colour

Base colour is dark grey; lips are very big, coloured in pink, with some dark pink vertical lines on them. The colour of the eyeballs are black on which white circular lines are present. Above and below the eyelid there are some yellow wavy lines. On either sides of the eyebrows, there are two broad wavy lines. The forehead of the mask is marked by some U-shaped black, pink, and yellow lines. The hair is light brown in colour, and corners of the eyes are red. The mask is meticulously coloured with blue, brown, white, grey, red and yellow to express its ferocity and tricky nature.

Mythology

Member of the shrewd, ferocious, and cruel mythological demon community, whose pleasure is to harass and punish all creatures, particularly gods and human beings.

Description

The demon looks very ferocious with untidy brown hair, which falls up to its shoulder. Face is very broad revealing the ugly teeth. The wide open eyes are very red as if blood is oozing out. With wrinkles on the forehead, the face looks very cruel and ferocious.

Sl. no.	:	14
Plate no.	:	42
Local name	:	*Danava / Rakshasha / Daitya* (II)
English equivalent	:	Demon
Type	:	*Mukh mukha*
Mask maker	:	Sri Koshakanta Deva Goswami (78 years)
Year of making	:	1996
Condition	:	Good
Maximum height	:	45 cm

Colour

The base of the mask is brown and red. Hair are golden brown; eyes are coloured with black, red, yellow, and white; nose and cheeks are brown with red patches; two big ears are brown, inner parts of which are red; jaws are red; both the perfect sets of teeth are ivory white.

Mythology

Same as Sl. No. 13

Description

The mask looks wicked and ferocious. The wide opened eyes and the mouth with a twisted flat nose express the duality of the demon's nature. On the middle of the forehead, there is a red spot under which there are six lunar-shaped marks which are alternately red and yellow. Hair on the head are golden and untidy; two broad ears are adorned with a pair of big, white earrings. Mouth is very broad, gums are red, and the two sets of beautiful teeth are sparkling white.

Sl. no.	:	15
Plate no.	:	43
Local name	:	*Danava / Rakshasha / Daitya* (III)
English equivalent	:	Demon
Type	:	*Mukh mukha*
Mask maker	:	Sri Hem Chandra Goswami (53 years)
Year of making	:	1996
Condition	:	Very good
Maximum height	:	42 cm

Colour

The base colour of the mask is blue. Eyeballs are black encircled by white spots. Eyebrows are black, below which yellow wavy lines are drawn. The colour of the lips is red with visible white teeth of the upper jaw. A round red spot is present on the forehead encircled by yellow lines above which a black line is drawn. The colour of the ears is blue.

Mythology

Same as Sl. No. 13

Description

The mask looks like that of a stout human being. The eyes are broad with beautifully drawn attractive eyebrows. A prominent spot is present at the middle of the forehead; lips are long and irregular in shape showing the teeth of upper jaw. Blue ears are elongated, inner side of which are red. The chin and nostrils of the mask are prominent.

Sl. no.	:	16
Plate no.	:	44
Local name	:	*Danava / Rakshasha / Daitya* (IV)
English equivalent	:	Demon
Type	:	*Mukh mukha*
Mask maker	:	Sri Hem Chandra Goswami (53 years)
Year of making	:	2001
Condition	:	Very good
Maximum height	:	25 cm

Colour

Base colour of the mask is brownish yellow; eyebrows and eyeballs are black in colour; the tip of the nose and nostrils are red and just above the nostrils, black arched lines are seen; the inner side of the eyelids is red in colour; eyelashes are black. On the forehead, one lunar-shaped spot is drawn from the middle of which an arrow mark runs over the nose. The lips and inner side of the ears are red. The two horns of the mask are in blackish maroon colour.

Mythology

Same as Sl. No. 13

Description

It is a beautiful mask, which possesses two sharp horns, akin to that of the bullock over its head. Through the wide open mouth, both the sets of teeth are visible; two teeth of the upper jaw are longer than the rest. The mask exhibits anger and cruelty.

Sl. no.	:	17
Plate no.	:	45
Local name	:	Dhenukasura
English equivalent	:	A demon that looks like a bull
Type	:	*Cho mukha* (only facial part is shown in the plate)
Mask maker	:	Sri Koshakanta Deva Goswami (78 years)
Year of making	:	1997
Condition	:	Very good
Maximum height	:	44 cm

Colour

Base of the mask is yellow; nostrils and lips are red; apex of the upper part of the mouth is dark blue; teeth and the surroundings of nostrils and eyes are bluish white; eyes are carefully drawn with black lines; bluish white lines are present adjacent to the eyebrows; zigzag, crosswise knitted black lines are present above the nose of the mask; black lines are drawn here and there of the face to make the mask attractive; brown colour hairs are present over the head.

Mythology

Dhenukasura (*dhenu* means bull/cow, and *asura* means demon) was a ferocious demon, who was killed by Balarama, the elder brother of Lord Krishna. Lord Krishna was the adopted son of Nanda, the king of a small kingdom, Gokula. He ruled over Yadava, a pastoral community. Nanda had two wives, Yasoda and Rohini. Balarama was the son of Rohini, and Krishna's foster mother was Yasoda. Being members of the pastoral community, Krishna and Balarama used to look after domesticated cattle along with their teenager friends. Once, while they took their cattle for grazing in the dense forest, they saw a tree full of ripe fruits. The cowherds picked some fruits of the tree belonging to Dhenukasura. The demon was angry at the action of the cowherds, and took the form of a bullock (*dhenu*). He ran to the spot and began to kick Balarama. The young hero seized the demon by the heels, whirled him round till he was dead, and cast his carcass on the top of a palm tree.

Description

It is a very attractive mask; looks more like a combination of heads of a cow and an ass. The eyes are akin to those of a human being. Over the head, a bunch of brown hair is present. Ears and upper part of the mouth resemble those of an ass. The mouth is open exhibiting the well set teeth of the lower jaw. Instead of ferocity, the mask expresses calm and quietness.

Sl. no.	:	18
Plate no.	:	46
Local name	:	Dundubhi
English equivalent	:	The demon Dundubhi
Type	:	*Mukh mukha*
Mask maker	:	Sri Hem Chandra Goswami (53 years)
Year of making	:	2006
Condition	:	Very good
Maximum height	:	56 cm

Colour

The base colour of the mask is dark grey and yellowish brown; eyebrows and eyeballs are black; eye lens are red; chin is greyish brown in colour, moustaches are black; lips and lower portion of the neck are red; the hairs are dark golden brown in colour; nose is greyish brown and inner side of the nostrils is red; teeth are dirty white, and earrings are yellow-red in colour. The spot on the forehead is red and white. Horns on the head are coloured black with white and yellow stripes.

Mythology

Dundubhi was a terrible and ferocious demon, the son of Maya danava, and the brother of Mayavi. Ravana was his brother-in-law. His form was like a buffalo with the strength of a thousand elephants. Proud and confident of his own prowess and losing his head for the boon he had received from Lord Siva, Dundubhi went about challenging whomsoever he met for a fight. Once he challenged Bali, the monkey king of Kiskindhya. The demon who possessed the body and horn of the buffalo, looking as dark as a terrible cloud in the sky, started roaring like hell at the tower gates of Kiskindhya. He started uprooting trees with his horn, and tearing the earth with his hoofs. Bali rush forth to engage Dundubhi in mortal duel, in which the former began gaining more and more strength due to his boon that when fighting someone from front, he would gain half the strength of the opponent. Dundubhi became weaker and weaker and flew away to a cave to save his life. Bali followed Dundubhi into the cave. In the cave, a great fight ensued in which Dundubhi was killed.

Description

The mask of Dundubhi expresses anger and ferocity. Eyes are prominent and wide open. Face is very broad, cheek bones and jaw bones are conspicuous. Nose is very large and nostrils are big and prominent. Moustaches are sparse and curled. Teeth show a more or less rectangular shape and two canine teeth are bigger and sharper; ears are large and earrings are circular in shape. The lower portion of the mask shows a cut mark, and is red in colour. Hair on the head are long and untidy; two horns similar to that of a buffalo are present above the head.

Sl. no.	:	19
Plate no.	:	47
Local name	:	Dushana
English equivalent	:	The demon Dushana
Type	:	*Mukh mukha*
Mask maker	:	Sri Hem Chandra Goswami (53 years)
Year of making	:	2006
Condition	:	Very good
Maximum height	:	41 cm

Colour

The base of the mask is beautifully coloured with brown and red; hair are dark brown in colour; eyebrows, eyeballs, and moustaches are black. The lips and inner side of the ears are red in colour; spot on the middle of the forehead is coloured white and red. The head band and earrings of the mask are beautifully coloured with yellow, red, and green.

Mythology

Dushana was one of the most ferocious and tricky demons of Lanka. He was the great associate of Ravana's brother Khara. This demon was also a general of Ravana, who fought with Rama and was killed by Rama.

Description

The mask of Dushana is beautifully ornamented with different embellishments. This mask expresses ferocity and anger. Head band of the mask is impressively coloured in red, yellow, and white with leaf-shaped structure and round raised spots. In between the two broad and continuous eyebrows of the mask, one prominent leafless tree-shaped spot coloured in red and white is drawn. The eyes are very big, and circular eyeballs convey ferocity. The nose is very big, flat with bulging nostrils. Moustaches are large, thick, black in colour which curl up to the cheeks of the face. The lips are reddish and horizontally elongated; ears of the mask are long, broad, with two earrings in each of them. The upper portion of the earrings is circular in shape, which is attached to the pinna of the ears, and the lower one, which is more or less elongated pitcher shaped, hangs from the upper one. Both the earrings are beautifully coloured in red, yellow, and green. The hair are untidy, dark brown in colour with two charming knots in right and left side of the neck.

Sl. no.	:	20
Plate no.	:	48
Local name	:	Hanumana
English equivalent	:	Hanumana, the mighty monkey warrior
Type	:	*Mukh mukha*
Mask maker	:	Sri Hem Chandra Goswami (53 years)
Year of making	:	2006
Condition	:	Very good
Maximum height	:	41 cm

Colour

The base colour of the mask is brown. The eyebrows, eyeballs, and eyelashes are black; arch-shaped golden yellow lines are drawn above and below the eyelids; lips are red; crown on the head is coloured golden yellow, red and black; the tidy hair of the mask is dark golden brown in colour.

Mythology

Hanumana was a monkey chief and son of Pavana (the wind god). In the *Ramayana,* Hanumana is an important character that is believed to have supernatural powers to fly and to jump from India to Sri Lanka in one bound crossing the vast sea. His size is believed to be like a mountain and as tall as a gigantic tower. His tail is very long and interminable. Once in Lanka, during a fight with Ravana and the demons, he was caught and his tail was greased and set to fire; but with his skill of flying, he set off the Lanka city on fire. He was a great devotee of Rama. He acted as a spy and fought most valiantly for Rama. He flew to the Himalayas to bring medicinal herb for the wounded Laksmana, killed monster Kalanemi, and thousands of others who assailed him. He was also a great grammarian.

Description

The face of the mask is round and looks calm and quiet. Eyes are big and prominent; the spot on the forehead is U-shaped and it is golden and red in colour. Nasal bridge is short; nasal septum is elongated and comes forward. Facial prognathism is well marked; lips are elongated and red. Hair on the face and head are very long and golden brown in colour. Ears are big and long. The crown on the head is very beautiful and it is decorated with meticulous floral designs.

Sl. no.	:	21
Plate no.	:	49
Local name	:	Jatayu
English equivalent	:	The mighty bird Jatayu
Type	:	*Mukh mukha*
Mask maker	:	Sri Hem Chandra Goswami (53 years)
Year of making	:	2005
Condition	:	Good
Maximum height	:	44 cm

Colour

The base colour of the mask is dirty white; eyes are black; the beak is pinkish red; the crest on the head is yellow and white in colour.

Mythology

Jatayu was a mighty bird who was believed to be the son of Garuda, the vehicle of Lord Vishnu; others believed that he was the son of Aruna (sun) and Syeni. He became an ally of Rama and clashed with Ravana, who was abducting Sita, and in a fierce fight that they fought in the air,

Ravana defeated Jatayu and cut off Jatayu's wings; Jatayu fell on earth, almost dead. Rama and Lakshmana during their search in the forest for Sita came across Jatayu who was lying almost dead without his wings, chanting Rama's name continuously. Jatayu told Rama about Ravana abducting Sita, and died. Rama and Lakshmana cremated Jatayu and the great bird's soul attained salvation.

Description

The mask of Jatayu looks innocent, calm and quiet. It looks like a typical bird with a beak opened and slightly curved outward. The eyes are prominent and round. Crest of the head is beautifully designed with yellow and white. The neck of the bird is thick and cylindrical.

Sl. no.	:	22
Plate no.	:	50
Local name	:	Khara
English equivalent	:	The demon Khara
Type	:	*Mukh mukha*
Mask maker	:	Sri Hem Chandra Goswami (53 years)
Year of making	:	2006
Condition	:	Very good
Maximum height	:	43 cm

Colour

The base colour of the mask is blue; eyebrows, eyeballs, and moustaches are black; lips and inner side of the eyelids and ears are red in colour. The turban of the head, spot mark on forehead, and earrings are beautifully coloured in yellow and red, and hairs are golden brown in colour.

Mythology

Khara was the son of demon Visravas and his wife Raka. He was twin brother of demon Surpanakha and half-brother of Ravana, the demon king of Lanka. Khara and Surpanakha stayed with the demon king Ravana, and his brothers Kumbhakarna, and Vibhisana, and served them. He was a ferocious and dangerous man-eating demon who was also an adept archer. During their stay in the forest of Dandakaranya, Rama, Sita and Laksmana were approached by Surpanakha, the sister of Khara. She tried her best to secure one of the brothers, either Rama or Laksmana, as her husband. Laksmana chopped off her nose and ears. She went to her well wishers Khara, Dusana, and Trisira and cried before them. The three demons immediately departed for Dandakaranya along with fourteen thousand giants to fight with Rama and Laksmana, but all of them were killed by the latter.

Description

The mask of Khara looks angry and excited. It has long brown hair with golden tinge. The top of the head is adorned with a beautifully designed turban of red and yellow colour. It has two long and broad ears adorned beautifully with two attractive earrings, which are coloured with red and yellow. The eyes are very big and prominent, and express ferocity. Moustaches are very long and thick, not continuous and absent in the middle portion of the upper lip; open ends of the moustaches are curled up on cheeks. The eyebrows are also broad and thick; black in colour, and just in between the two eyebrows, on the forehead, a meticulously drawn multicolour spot is seen. The nose of the mask is broad, long, pointed, and nostrils are oval shaped. Mouth is wide open showing two sets of irregular teeth and red tongue.

Sl. no.	:	23
Plate no.	:	51
Local name	:	Kumbhakarna
English equivalent	:	The demon *Kumbha* (pitcher) *karna* (ears)
Type	:	*Cho mukha* (only facial part is shown in the plate)
Mask maker	:	Sri Hem Chandra Goswami (53 years)
Year of making	:	2006
Condition	:	Very good
Maximum height	:	1.5 mt

Colour

Base colour of the mask is chocolate brown; the lips, tongue, inner side of the nostrils, and ears are red in colour; eyebrows are black, and just below the eyebrows two wavy yellow lines are drawn; the eyelashes and moustaches are dark brown; teeth are ivory white; ears are pinkish brown in colour and on the pinna of them two rings of yellow, white, and red colours are seen; the crown on the head is beautifully coloured in yellow, red, pink, and white; hair is of dark brown colour, and the spot on the middle of the forehead is beautifully coloured in yellow, red and white.

Mythology

Kumbha (pitcher) *karna* (ears) was the powerful brother of the demon-king Ravana, who was well known for his excessive sleeping habit. His father was Visravasa, and mother was Kesini. It was believed that under the curse of Lord Brahma, the creator, he could sleep for six long months at a stretch in a year. Facing a great difficulty to fight with Rama, Ravana sent his associates to arouse Kumbhakarna. This was followed by great efforts of the associates with beating drums, conch, flute, etc. near the ears of the demon Kumbhakarna while he was sleeping. After much difficulties, he woke up and drinking two thousand jars of liquor he went to his brother Ravana, and afterwards took the battlefield against the monkey army, headed by Rama. He defeated monkey chief Sugriva with a large stone and carried him into the city of Lanka as a prisoner. After that he returned to the battlefield and encountered Rama. After a long and fierce battle with Rama, he was defeated and Rama cut off his head.

Description

The mask of Kumbhakarna is very attractive and beautiful. It is adorned with golden yellow crown on the top of which some floral designs are drawn in red, white, and yellow colour. One horizontal zigzag band is also seen in the middle portion of the crown with crossed linen in white over red. The eyes are very big and prominent with eyeballs encircling brown concentric lines. The upper parts of the eyelids are movable with the help of which eyes can be opened and closed. The eyelashes are very long, beautiful, and dark brown in colour. Nose of the mask is flat and broad, while the top of it is pointed; inner side of nostrils are red. The moustaches are very big, coarse, and curl up to the cheeks of the face. The mouth is widely open and very big in size. Teeth are ivory white in colour; five pointed teeth of upper jaw are seen coming outward. The lips, gums, and the tongue are red in colour. Lower portion of the chin is movable. The ears of the mask are adorned with two meticulously made attractive earrings. The spot on forehead is seen as two overlapping inscriptions, which are horizontally elongated ring and vertically U shaped, in the lower curve of which one white coloured flame is drawn.

Sl. no.	:	24
Plate no.	:	52

Local name	:	Maricha (I)
English equivalent	:	The demon Maricha
Type	:	*Mukh mukha*
Mask maker	:	Sri Hem Chandra Goswami (53 years)
Year of making	:	1998
Condition	:	Slightly distorted
Maximum height	:	40 cm

Colour

The base of the mask is blue and green. The eyeballs are black in colour surrounded by red circles. Green and yellow lines are drawn upward and downward from the eyelids. Just below the eyelids there are some small black lines to give the impression of eyelashes. Hair on the head are light brown in colour and on either side of the head one horn is present, which is black in colour. Blue coloured lips are irregular in shape. Teeth are coloured white and gums are red. On the forehead of the mask there is red coloured, V-shaped signs encircled by yellow lines, in the middle of which a circular spot; the cheeks are yellowish green in colour, the colour of the ears are blue, inner side of which are red; two circular pinkish white earrings are present in the earlobes of the mask.

Mythology

Maricha, the son of ferocious demon Taraka, was the maternal uncle of Ravana (see Ravana in this chapter), the powerful king of the demon kingdom Lanka. Maricha was a minister of the Ravana's court, who expertised in deceit magic, the worldly illusion, to mislead mankind. When Rama, the eldest prince of Ayodhya kingdom, was in exile in the dense forest Dandakaranya with his wife Sita and brother Lakshmana, Surpanakha (see Surpanakha in this chapter) was charmed by the beauty and strength of Rama and Lakshmana, and tried to marry them. As a punishment Lakshmana cut her nose and ears. Surpanakha returned to Lanka and informed Ravana that in Dandakaranya there was a beautiful lady who was fit to be the wife of Ravana. She also informed that while she tried to take the woman for Ravana, her associates punished her by cutting her nose and ears. Enraged, Ravana vowed to punish Rama and Lakshmana by abducting Sita. According to the conspiracy of Ravana, Maricha took the form of a golden deer to inveigle Sita. Sita was charmed by the beauty of the golden deer and asked Rama to catch the animal. Rama went out from the cottage to catch the deer and when he failed to catch it alive, killed the animal. At the time of death, deer-shaped Maricha shouted Lakshmana in the voice of Rama to save him. On the request of Sita, Lakshmana went out to save Rama. Sita was alone in the cottage. Ravana took the shape of a hermit and asked Sita for alms. When Sita came out from the cottage, Ravana resumed his own form and carried away Sita.

Description

The mask possesses two broad eyes and flat nose with large nostrils; open mouth showing two sets of sparkling teeth; two large earrings in elongated ears; two horns amidst untidy golden hair; horns resemble that of the bullocks; the mask expresses shrewdness and ferocity.

Sl. no.	:	25
Plate no.	:	53
Local name	:	Maricha (II)
English equivalent	:	The demon Maricha
Type	:	*Mukh mukha*
Mask maker	:	Sri Kosakanta Deva Goswami (78 years)
Year of making	:	1997
Condition	:	Very good
Maximum height	:	43 cm

Colour

Base of the mask is brown. The eyeballs are black and in the middle two concentric white circular marks are there. The corners of the eyes are red; eyebrows are black in colour arranged in zigzag manner, which looks like continuous cross marks. Above the nostrils two continuous wavy white and black lines are drawn, which run up to the mouth. The lips are pink in colour and are very broad and elongated. The teeth are irregularly arranged and are dirty white in colour. The gums are red. One prominent spot is on the middle of the forehead, which is coloured with black, red, and white. The hair of the mask is grey in colour.

Mythology

Same as Sl. no. 24

Description

It is a beautiful mask which expresses anger and cruelty. Meticulously drawn eyes are obliquely placed, over which eyebrows are drawn by continuous cross marks. A lotus petal shaped spot is there on the forehead at the middle of the eyebrows. Ears are very big. The head is covered with whitish brown hair, and at the middle of the head, a small hair knot is present. The nose is pointed. The mouth is very broad and open showing two sets of teeth.

Sl. no.	:	26
Plate no.	:	54
Local name	:	Mayavi
English equivalent	:	Mayavi, the demon
Type	:	*Mukh mukha*
Mask maker	:	Sri Hem Chandra Goswami (53 years)
Year of making	:	2006
Condition	:	Very good
Maximum height	:	45 cm

Colour

The base colour of the mask is purple white. Eyebrows and eyeballs are black; just below the eyebrows there is a yellow line; the lips and inner side of the nostrils are red. Teeth are ivory white; earrings are coloured in yellow and red; hair of the head are dark brown and horns are black; the beads hanging from horns are red and yellow in colour.

Mythology

Mayavi was a ferocious demon and an expert magician. He was the son of Mayadanava, the great architect of the demons and his mother was Hema, a nymph. Mayadanava had two sons, Mayavi and Dundubhi. Mayavi was very courageous, who liked to fight with anybody without any cause. Once he challenged Bali, the mighty monkey king of Kiskindhya. Bali defeated Mayavi who ran away from Bali and hid himself in a big cave. Bali followed him and ultimately killed him.

Description

The mask of this tricky demon expresses ferocity and wickedness. Face is irregular in shape; eyes are big, prominent, and wide open; eyebrows are untidy; spot on the forehead is more or less V-shaped coloured in red and yellow; Lips are thick, elevated, and uneven in shape; teeth are regular in shape with two pointed teeth in the upper jaw. The lower jaw of the mask is movable. The earrings are circular in shape, hair on the head is untidy and long. Two horns akin to those of buffalo are present on forehead from the tip of which two circular bids coloured in red and yellow are hanging.

Sl. no.	:	27
Plate no.	:	55
Local name	:	Narasimgha (I)
English equivalent	:	Combination of man (*nara*) and lion (*Singha*)
Type	:	*Cho mukha* (only upper part of the mask is shown in the plate)
Mask maker	:	Sri Hem Chandra Goswami (53 years)
Year of making	:	1999
Condition	:	Very good
Maximum height	:	2 mt (in the plate only the upper part of the mask is seen)

Colour

Base colour of the mask is white and yellow; eyebrows and eyeballs are black in colour; below the eyebrows and above each eyelid one golden wavy line is drawn; the colour of inner side of the eyelids and gums is red; the tongue of the mask is blackish red in colour; inner side of nostrils are red, and above and below them some black lines are drawn. Eyelashes are black in colour and are artistically drawn from both sides of the eye corner up to the ear and nostrils of the mask. The teeth are white in colour. In the upper part of the neck, one feather-like structure is present which is coloured in green, yellow, and red. The mane of the mask is coloured with golden yellow, white, and green. The ears are white with red inner side. In the base of the ear, some circles in golden, red, black and green colours are drawn.

Mythology

Nara (man) *simha* (lion) or Narasingha means 'the man-lion'. Lord Vishnu assumed this form to deliver the world from the tyranny of Hiranyakasipu, a demon, who with the boon of Lord Brahma (the creator) had become invulnerable, and was secure from gods, men, and animals. This demon's son, named Prahlada, worshipped Vishnu, which so incensed his father that he tried to kill him, but his efforts were all in vain. Contending with his son as to the omnipotence and omnipresence of Lord Vishnu, Hiranyakasipu demanded to know if Vishnu was present in the stone pillar of his court, and struck it violently. To avenge the fortune on Prahlada, and to vindicate his own offended majesty, Vishnu came forth from the pillar as the Narasimha, half-lion half-man animal, and tore the arrogant demon king to pieces.

Description

It is a very attractive mask made on the basis of one of the principal Vaishnavite scriptures, the *Kirtana*. The base colour of the mask is white. On the elongated cylindrical neck, the head of a lion is placed. The two long and pointed ears closely resemble those of the horse. Eyes are very beautifully drawn and akin to that of a woman. In the open mouth, two perfect sets of teeth along with four long canines are prominent. The tongue is very long and red in colour. Just below the head, the neck is meticulously adorned with two golden necklaces. Artistic mane is golden yellow in colour. Broadly open mouth and stretched out long red tongue express ferocity.

Sl. no.	:	28
Plate no.	:	56
Local name	:	Narasimha (II)
English equivalent	:	Combination of man (*nara*) and lion (*simha*)
Type	:	*Cho mukha* (only the upper part of the mask is shown in the plate)
Mask maker	:	Sri Koshakanta Deva Goswami (78 years)
Year of making	:	2006
Condition	:	Very good
Maximum height	:	1.75 mt

Colour

Basic colour is white; crown and ornaments are golden; tongue and nails are red; body and waist bands are red with golden floral designs, while the body is tinged with sky blue.

Mythology

Same as Sl. no. 27

Description

An attractive mask of the Narasimha incarnation of Lord Vishnu, it possesses four strong hands with meticulously carved fingers and pointed nails, the neck of the mask is very long and does not resemble with that of a lion, but the facial part resembles to that of a lion; ears are pointed; mouth is open showing the long tongue and two sets of teeth; two canines of the upper jaw are long and pointed. Neck, hands, and the waist are adorned with meticulously designed ornaments; the robust body exhibits the vigour of Narasimha.

Sl. no.	:	29
Plate no.	:	57
Local name	:	Nila
English equivalent	:	The monkey chief Nila
Type	:	*Mukh mukha*
Mask maker	:	Sri Hem Chandra Goswami (51 years)
Year of making	:	2005
Condition	:	Good
Maximum height	:	43 cm

Colour

The base colour of the mask is light purple and pinkish brown; lips and inner side of the nostrils are pink; eyelids are pinkish brown, and inner side of those are red. The head band on the forehead is yellow and red in colour; ears are blackish orange and inner side of those is red. Hair on the head and face are brown; teeth of the mask are white in colour.

Mythology

Nila was a monkey chief and son of the god of fire, Agni. He shone forth like *agni* (fire). He was one of the most effulgent, reputed, and powerful figure among the monkey army who assisted Sri Rama in his war with the demon king Ravana. In the Rama-Ravana war, Nila killed Pramathi, the younger brother of the demon called Dusana. He was also one of the ardent devotees and followers of Sri Rama.

Description

The mask of Nila is a typical monkey mask. A well-marked facial prognathism is seen in the mask, which is a characteristic feature of the apes. The forehead is slant, ears are circular; stripe on the forehead is yellow and red in colour; eyes are smaller; nose is short and tip of the nose is pointed; hair on the head and faces are long and untidy. Nila's mask in general expresses anger and excitement.

Sl. no.	:	30
Plate no.	:	58
Local name	:	Pralambasura
English equivalent	:	Pralamba, the demon
Type	:	*Mukh mukha*
Mask maker	:	Sri Prasanna Goswami (41 years)
Year of making	:	2001
Condition	:	Very good
Maximum height	:	42 cm

Colour

The base colour of the mask is reddish brown. The eyebrows and eyeballs are black in colour. Inner sides of the eyelids are red and eyelashes are drawn with red and yellow colour. The outer side of the eyelids is coloured with yellow and black. The lips are pink and encircled in black lines. Gums are also pink and the teeth are white in colour. Hair are grey. The colour of the ears are brown, inner side of which is painted red.

Mythology

Pralamba was a violent demon and is one of the associates of Kamsa, the maternal uncle of Krishna, and the king of Mathura. It was known by Kamsa that he would be killed by Krishna. So he tried his best to destroy Krishna. He sent Pralambasura to kill Krishna along with Krishna's brother Balarama by any means. With the object of devouring both Krishna and Balarama, Pralambasura teamed up with them as one of the members of playgroup in jumping. Pralambasura was beaten by his opponent Balarama, and according to the rules of the game had to carry the winner back on his shoulder to the starting place. He took up Balarama and then expanded his form, and was making off with his rider when Balarama called upon Krishna for assistance. Krishna made a long speech, and ended by telling him to suspend a while his mortal character, and do what was right. Balarama laughed and squeezed Pralambasura with his knees, and beat him on the head with his fists till his eyes were knocked out and his brain forced through his skull, so that he fell to the ground and died.

Description

The mask of Pralambasura is very beautiful, which expresses mischievousness along with cruelty. The artist made it very meticulously and every part of the mask like eyes, nose, cheeks, lips, mouth, teeth, etc. express the turbulent nature of the demon.

Sl. no.	:	31
Plate no.	:	59
Local name	:	Ravana (I)
English equivalent	:	The demon king Ravana
Type	:	*Cho mukha* (only facial part is shown in the plate)
Mask maker	:	Sri Hem Chandra Goswami (53 years)

Year of making	:	2002
Condition	:	Arms and body parts are destroyed; crowns of the additional heads are slightly damaged
Maximum height	:	1.5 mt; head 26.3 cm

Colour

The base colour of the mask is blue. Hair, eyebrows, eyeballs, and moustache are black in colour. Lips and inner side of the ears are red. Just above the eyebrows, two golden feather-shaped impressions are painted. On the middle of the forehead, a black colour trident (*trisul*) shaped mark is present. The crown of the main head and earrings are golden in colour.

Mythology

Ravana was the demon-king of Lanka (Sri Lanka). His subjects were known as *rakshasas*. By penance and worship to Lord Brahma, the creator, Ravana became invulnerable against gods and men, but he was doomed to die through a woman. He was described in the *Ramayana* as having ten heads, twenty arms, copper coloured eyes, and bright teeth like the young moon. His form was like a thick cloud or a mountain or the god of death with open mouth. He had all the marks of royalty, but his body bore the impression of wounds inflicted by all divine arms in his warfare with the gods. His strength was so great that he could agitate the seas, and split the tops of mountains. He stopped with his arms the sun and moon in their course, and prevented their rising. To resist Ravana, Lord Vishnu, the protector, became incarnate as Rama. Sita was the beautiful wife of Rama. Rama's war against the demons inflicted great loss to them as to incense Ravana. Burning with rage, and excited by the passion for Sita, he abducted Sita. Rama sought the assistance of Sugriva and Hanumana, two monkey heroes, with their hosts of monkeys and bears. In a ferocious battle, Rama killed Ravana and rescued Sita. Ravana, though he was chief among demons, was a Brahmana on his father's side. He was well-versed in Sanskrit, observed the Vedic rituals, and was an adept sitarist. His character projects an uncommon mixture of good and evil.

Description

It is a surprisingly beautiful mask where nine smaller heads are arranged in a semi-circular manner with the main head. All the heads possess thick black eyebrows and moustaches, broad and long eyes and crimson lips; flat nose with pointed tips; prominent muscle at the back of the chin of main head; long curly black hair; trident-shaped spot on the middle of the forehead of main head; base of the trident has floral design; a U-shaped mark drawn with white and black stripes from the root of nose to the middle of the forehead envelopes the trident; base of the trident is adorned with a lotus petal shaped mark; border of the petal is drawn in black, middle of it is white; there is meticulous decoration over the eyebrows of the principal head; all heads are adorned with beautiful crowns; the crown of the main head is golden in colour; other crowns are white-based and decorated with golden and red marks; the main head bears conspicuous earrings of golden colour; the lips of the principal head are slightly open exhibiting the sparkling and well arranged beautiful teeth of upper jaw; additional heads are tinged with smiles; the main head expresses pride and self content.

Sl. no.	:	32
Plate no.	:	60
Local name	:	Ravana (II)
English equivalent	:	Ravana, the demon king
Type	:	*Cho mukha* (only facial part is shown in the plate)
Mask maker	:	Sri Hem Chandra Goswami (53 years)
Year of making	:	2006
Condition	:	Very good

Colour

The base colour is blue; broad eyes and eyebrows are drawn in black; eye balls are black surrounded by white with tinges of yellow and red; lips are red; moustaches are black; ears are adorned with beautiful ear ornaments basically of golden colour. The crowns are golden in colour.

Mythology

Same as Sl. no. 31

Description

The attractive mask expresses uncertainty and agony of life. With the principal head, nine identical heads are arranged in a semi-circular manner. All the heads are adorned with crowns; the crown of the main head is meticulously designed. The heads have black, long, and beautiful eyes, and thick well-curved eyebrows; moustaches are thick, black, and curvy. Forehead is adorned with U-shaped red spot encircled on the upper part by two oval marks; the spot comes down to the root of the nose; beautiful ears possess eye-catching ornaments, which are principally divided into two parts; upper part is like a round flower, and the lower part is like a conical bud; the nose is broad but pointed showing distinctly oblique nostrils; lips are broad and red, bordered by blue lines.

Sl. no.	:	33
Plate no.	:	61
Local name	:	Ravana (III)
English equivalent	:	Ravana, the demon king
Type	:	*Cho mukha* (only facial part is shown in the plate)
Mask maker	:	Sri Koshakanta Deva Goswami (78 years)
Year of making	:	2005
Condition	:	Very good
Maximum height	:	1.5 mt

Colour

The basic colour of the mask is blue; eyeballs, eyebrows and moustaches are black; crowns and ear ornaments are golden; in the crowns some parts are coloured in red; teeth are ivory white, and lips are red.

Mythology

Same as Sl. No. 31

Description

It is a very attractive mask expressing vigour and pride. As usual, nine heads are arranged in a semi-circular manner by the principal head; all the heads are adorned with beautiful crowns of golden and red colour; the forehead is decorated with U-shaped spot in the middle of which an arrow mark is present. Thick and curved moustaches add arrogance to the personality of the demon-king Ravana.

Sl. no.	:	34
Plate no.	:	62
Local name	:	Ravana (*Bhikharirupi)*
English equivalent	:	Ravana in the disguise of a beggar
Type	:	*Mukh mukha*
Mask maker	:	Sri Hem Chandra Goswami (53 years)

Year of making	:	2005
Condition	:	Very good
Maximum height	:	32 cm

Colour

The face colour of the mask is greenish brown; hair and moustaches are golden in colour; lips are red and teeth are white; brown eyebrows are segmented by oblique white marks.

Mythology

The mask depicts Ravana when he in the guise of a beggar and begged for alms from Sita, who was in exile with her husband Rama and his brother Lakshmana. At that time Sita was alone in the cottage. When Sita came out to give alms to the beggar, Ravana abducted Sita (for details see Ravana in this chapter).

Description

The mask represents a down-trodden man's face expressing greediness and mischievousness. Head is partially without hair; hairs and moustaches are untidy; eyes are beautiful but not identical; nose is flat and nostrils are wide; mouth is opened showing the teeth of the upper jaw.

Sl. no.	:	35
Plate no.	:	63
Local name	:	Sankhachura
English equivalent	:	Sankha, the demon
Type	:	*Mukh mukha*
Mask maker	:	Sri Hem Chandra Goswami (53 years)
Year of making	:	2001
Condition	:	Very good
Maximum height	:	25.5 cm

Colour

Base colour of the mask is brownish yellow. The hair, eyebrows, and moustaches are black in colour. Eyeballs are black encircled by yellow concentric rings. The inner side of the eyelids and nostrils are pink in colour. The lips are pink, outer lining of which is black; teeth are ivory white. On the forehead two elongated spots in black and red are painted. Over the base of the nose, a petal-shaped red and black colour spot is also there.

Mythology

Sankhachura was a ferocious demon. After receiving a boon from god he became more turbulent. His wife Tulasi was a very pious lady and according to the boon, only if the chastity of Tulasi could be molested, only then Sankhachura could be killed. To get rid of the atrocities of Sankhachura, Lord Vishnu took the shape of Sankhachura and molested the modesty of Tulasi. Due to this act of Vishnu, Sankhachura lost all his power and strength. Finally, Lord Vishnu killed Sankhachura.

Description

The mask of Sankhachura expresses anger and excitement. It has untidy black hair on head and two elongated ears adorned with a pair of ear ornament. Eyes are widely open, over which thick and black eyebrows are present. The nose is very flat with conspicuous nostrils, under which a thick and long moustache is present. Through widely open mouth-sharp teeth of both the jaws are visible; a few teeth are longer than the others. The middle of the forehead is decorated with a pair of spots.

Sl. no.	:	36
Plate no.	:	64
Local name	:	Simgha
English equivalent	:	Lion (only the facial part is shown in the plate)
Type	:	*Cho mukha*
Mask maker	:	Sri Koshakanta Deva Goswami (78 years)
Year of making	:	1998
Condition	:	Very good
Maximum height	:	40 cm

Colour

The base colour of the mask is brown; eyebrows and eyeballs are black in colour; nose is pink, inner side of which is red. The inner part of the eyelids and gums of the teeths are also red. On the chin some wavy black and white lines are drawn. Beards of the mask are coloured in black and white. The hairs and the mane are grey in colour.

Description

The mask closely resembles a lion; manes are grey; eyes are aggressive; flat nose possesses two wide nostrils; mouth is widely open showing four sharp long teeth along with other shorter teeth of upper and lower jaw.

Sl. no.	:	37
Plate no.	:	65
Local name	:	Sugriva
English equivalent	:	The monkey king Sugriva
Type	:	*Mukh mukha*
Mask maker	:	Sri Hem Chandra Goswami (53 years)
Year of making	:	2006
Condition	:	Very good
Maximum height	:	43 cm

Colour

The base of the mask is pinkish brown; eyebrows, eyeballs and eyelashes are black in colour; below the eyebrows, a yellow coloured line is drawn; tip of the nose and lips are pink in colour. The hairs and beard on the face are golden brown. Earrings on the ears are red and golden yellow; inside of the ears is red. The crown on the head is yellow and red.

Mythology

Su (means handsome) and *griva* (neck), so Sugriva was the monkey king of Kiskindhya with beautiful neck. He was believed to be the son of the sun and so he was known as Ravi-nandana (son of men) and other similar names. He was endowed with the capacity to change his form at will. He was helpful and never hesitated to help his friends. His wife's name was Ruma. It is said that once he was dethroned by his own brother Bali. Rama helped him in war against Bali and re-installed him at the throne. Sugriva along with his adviser Hanumana and their monkey army was an ally of Rama in war against Ravana. In that war Sugriva was wounded by Ravana's brother Kumbhakarna.

Description

The mask of Sugriva is very charming, and a well decorated one. The crown on the head is bright golden yellow and reddish. On its top the inverted U-shaped structure is in red and white. The eyebrows are very prominent. The eyes are also very big, and wide open. The mask tells of the calm and quiet nature of the character. The nose is short and prominent. Prognathism is well marked on the face. Golden brown coloured hairs and beard on the face are beautifully attached to the mask. Two circular earrings along with a circular tip at the base of the rings in red and golden yellow makes the mask more impressive to look at. Overall, the expression of the face of the mask is that of a typical monkey.

Sl. no.	:	38
Plate no.	:	66
Local name	:	Surpanakha
English equivalent	:	Demoness Surpanakha
Type	:	*Mukh mukha*
Mask maker	:	Sri Hem Chandra Goswami (53 years)
Year of making	:	2000
Condition	:	Good

Colour

The base colour of the mask is blue; eyeballs, eyebrows and eyelashes are black in colour; lips and inner side of eyelids and ears are red in colour. On the forehead of the mask, three balck lunar-shaped lines are there. The hair are greenish black in colour and the earrings of the mask are yellow; teeth are irregular in shape and white in colour.

Mythology

The term Supranakha means having nails (*nakha*) like winnowing fan (*surpa*). She was a wicked and ferocious demoness and was the sister of Ravana, the demon-king of Lanka. Surpanakha was charmed by the beauty and strength of Rama and she fell in love with him. When she made advances, Rama sent her to Lakshmana, his brother, and Lakshmana in like manner sent her to back to Rama. Enraged at this double rejection, she fell upon Sita and Rama was obliged to interfere forcibly for the protection of his wife Sita. He ordered Lakshmana to disfigure the violent demoness, and Lakshmana chopped off her nose and ears. She flew to her brother Ravana for revenge, and this brought on the war between Rama and Ravana. She told Ravana about the beauty of Sita, and instigated him to abduct her.

Description

Surpanakha's mask expresses anger and ferocity; her hair are untidy, eyes are wide open, and her open mouth exhibits two sets of distorted teeth; both her ears are adorned with two big earrings; tip of the nose of the mask is detachable.

Sl. no.	:	39
Plate no.	:	67
Local name	:	Taraka
English equivalent	:	The demoness Taraka
Type	:	*Mukh mukha*

Mask maker	:	Sri Koshakanta Deva Goswami (78 years)
Year of making	:	2004
Condition	:	Very good
Maximum height	:	44 cm

Colour

The base coloure of the mask is purple; hair are golden in colour; eyebrows are black; eye pupil is black with a circular white ring inside each of it; inner sides of the eyelids are red; the colour of nose is purple and sides of the nostrils are red; outer sides of those are encircled by a black circular line; lips are red and gum of the teeth are pink; teeth are dirty white. Chin is purple and some wavy lines in yellow and black are on it; ears are purpule on which some black and white lines are drawn. The inside of ears is red in colour. The earrings are beautifully coloured in yellow and red.

Mythology

Taraka was a ferocious demoness and mother of Maricha. She was transformed into a demoness because of a curse of the sage Agastya. She resided in a forest near the confluence of the river Sarju and carried on her atrocities all around the country. Sage Viswamitra desired Rama to kill her. Rama cut off her two arms so that she could be deprived of her magical power. Laksmana cut off her nose and ears. She, with the help of her sorcery, attacked Rama and Lakshmana with a deadly shower of stones. At last, Rama killed this dreaded demoness with the help of Viswamitra with an arrow.

Description

The mask of Taraka captures her blood thirst and angry nature. The eyes of the mask are prominent, widely open and express her ferocity; the nose is very broad and nostrils are circular and widely open. The face is disharmonious with prominent cheek and jaw bones. Lips are very broad and irregular in shape. Mouth is widely open with irregularly arranged teeth, inside which one half-eaten human figure is seen. The gum of the teeth is pink; ears are robust and rectangular in shape. On the pinna of ear, two drum-shaped rings are there. The hairs are very long and untidy.

Sl. no.	:	40
Plate no.	:	68
Local name	:	Tarakasura

English equivalent	:	The demon Tarakasura
Type	:	*Mukh mukha*
Mask maker	:	Sri Koshakanta Deva Goswami (78 years)
Year of making	:	2001
Condition	:	Good
Maximum height	:	39 cm

Colour

The base colour of the mask is blue and green; eyebrows are grey in colour, and just between the eyebrows on the forehead, one more or less circular spot of white and yellow colour is seen; eyeballs are black and inner side of eyelids are red in colour. The eyelids are surrounded by black, white, and yellow lines. Nose, chin, and cheek are green. Lips, gum, inner sides of nostrils, and ears are drawn with red colour.

Mythology

Tarakasura was the son of Vajranaka. He was a turbulent and ferocious demon and this demon's austerities made him formidable to the gods. For the destruction of Tarakasura, Kartika, the son of Lord Siva, was miraculously born, who ultimately killed the notorious demon.

Description

The mask possesses two broad eyes and a distorted nose with two wide and prominent nostrils. Ears are very big in comparison to the face; distorted mouth is widely open exhibiting the teeth of the upper jaw. At the middle of the forehead, there is an almost circular spot, upper half of which is yellow and the lower half is white.

Sl. no.	:	41
Plate no.	:	69
Local name	:	Trisira
English equivalent	:	The demon Trisira
Type	:	*Mukh mukha*
Mask maker	:	Sri Hem Chandra Goswami (53 years)
Year of making	:	2006
Condition	:	Very good
Maximum height	:	Middle 46 cm, the other two 42 cm each

Colour

Base colour of the mask is whitish brown; eyebrows, eyeballs, and eyelashes are black; just below the eyebrows, yellow lines are drawn; the inner side of eyelids and ears are red; lips and nostrils from inside are red; spots on the forehead are drawn in a combination of red and yellow colour; hair on the head and moustaches are dark brown.

Mythology

The Trisira (three-headed demon; *tri* means three, and *sira* means head) was a ferocious demon and a good friend of Ravana, the demon-king of Lanka. When Lakshmana during their exile in Dandakranya cut off the nose and ears of Surpanakha (sister of demon-king Ravana), the Khara, Dusana, and Trisira's combination led the attack on Rama. Trisira was a very brave and powerful fighter and Rama's forehead was injured by an arrow from Trisira. The latter came and fought in a chariot drawn by four horses. Ultimately, Trisira was killed by Rama.

Description

The mask of Trisira expresses ferocity and anger. Size of the middle head is larger than the other two heads. The eyes of all the three heads are very big in size and wide open. Eyeballs are circular and black; ears are very big and inner side of those are red; earrings on the pinna are small, circular and black in colour. The noses are broad, flat, pointed at tip, and nostrils are prominent. On the forehead region, two elongated spots of red and yellow colour is persisted. The moustaches of the middle head are larger and sparser than those of the other two; hair on the heads are untidy and dark brown in colour.

From the foregoing description, it is evident that at present there are only 41 masks available in Natun Chamaguri Satra. Most of the masks are in good condition; the slightly damaged ones are occasionally repaired and repainted. The masks which are badly damaged are thrown away in the nearby water sources. In this process, the masks of Narasimha, Ravana, etc. are immersed in the nearby river with great reverence by playing drums, cymbals, etc. and singing Vaishnavite hymns by a group of the villagers. The masks of demons overwhelmingly outnumber the masks of gods, animals, and human beings. All the masks are made by only four mask makers who are direct male descendents of the founder *satradhikar* of the Chamaguri Satra. The age of the eldest mask maker is 78 years, while the youngest one is 40 years of age. There are a few young mask makers in the study *satra*; but for non-availability of their masks, in the *satra* their works could not be included here. Their masks are bought by the tourists, particularly by the foreign tourists. Some of the masks like those of Baraha, Rakshasa, Ravana, etc. are found more than one in number.

Obviously, the different pieces of these masks of a single character show close affinity because their makers abided by the code of scriptures and strictly followed the tradition. Some of the masks have movable chin, eyelids, mouth, lower jaw, etc. Masks of the common demons are conspicuous for their expression, shrewdness, and cruelty. However, owing to the influence of Vaishnavism, the masks of mighty the Garuda, Ravana, etc. express rather piety and coyness instead of pride and cruelty. The masks made in Natun Chamaguri Satra are easily identified by the Hindus in general, and the Assamese in particular, because they are made on the basis of the descriptions given in scriptures and these people are familiar with them. Moreover, the makers and the viewers live in the same cultural environment.

6

Conclusion

In the preceding chapters, an attempt has been made to delineate the mask making tradition of Majuli in general and that of the Natun Chamaguri Satra in particular. It has been found that the *satras* of Majuli are rich in the art and skill of mask making, which have been handed down to them from one generation to the next. In this process of transmission, the mask making has lost some of the pristine traits, but have acquired some new elements. In this context, an endeavour has been made to examine the mask making tradition of the riverine island Majuli with special reference to Natun Chamaguri Satra where it is still a living tradition.

From time immemorial, Majuli has been a nucleus of Vaishnavism in this remote part of India. Sankaradeva, the founder and the principal preacher of Vaishnavite cult in North-East India, took Majuli as one of the main centres for its propagation amongst the people of different castes and tribes of the region. Sankaradeva established the first *satra* at Dhuvahat Belguri of Majuli, and in course of time many other *satras* were set up in different parts of Assam. In the hey days of the great guru Sankaradeva, there were 65 *satras* in Majuli; however, owing to various reasons, primarily for the recurrent devastating flood, at present there are only 22 *satras*, among which a good number are in a dilapidated condition. According to an estimate, there are 650 *satras* in Assam with thousands of devotees in and outside the state associated with these *satras*. The *satra* is a living institution in Assam, and apart from nourishing Vaishnavism, it has also enriched the composite culture of the entire region with its unique contribution in the diverse fields of art and culture. Masks are essential in *satra* culture. In Assamese form of Vaishnavism, one-act ritualistic plays are integral to the various festivals of the *satras* and the use of masks in those plays is indispensable. At present there are only four *satras* at Majuli, viz., Alengi Narasimha Satra, Bihimpur Satra, Natun Chamaguri Satra, and Prachin Chamaguri Satra, which have still kept alive the glorious tradition of mask making, and of these four *satras*, the Natun Chamaguri Satra has certainly achieved the highest degree of perfection of that skill. The masks made in the Natun Chamaguri Satra bewitch the beholders by their beauty. Art critics in and outside the state have highly praised these masks for their techniques and aesthetic beauty. Most of the mask makers of this *satra* have received different prestigious state and national awards and artist pensions. The material collected for the present study has been organized in six chapters of this thesis. Barring the conclusion, the other five chapters are devoted to the systematic arrangement of the collected material. In the Introduction, a brief discussion has been made on masks with special reference to that of Assam. The chapter also includes an account of the ethnographic scenario, objectives of the present study, methodology used and such other relevant things. Chapter II, i.e., 'Mask in the Context of Culture', delineates the available literature on masks. It has been observed that most of the data integral to the masks of different cultures are incorporated to the study of material culture, and a proper study on different dimensions of mask as thrust area is very scanty. In the Chapter III, an attempt has been made to focus on the general characteristics and various uses of mask. The principal use of a mask is to hide the identity of a person and to project him as another being. But masks have been used in many different ways by many different people. They have been used by primitive tribes to propitiate ancestors, deities and demons, and to assist in the rites of initiation of boys to manhood. Masks have been used for disciplinary, commemorative, therapeutic, and funerary purposes too. Theatrical uses of masks are common. In some societies, masks have been used to fulfil more than one purpose simultaneously.

The masks made in the Natun Chamaguri Satra are closely connected to the Vaishnavite theatrical performance known as *ankia bhaona* commonly known as *bhaona*. Laude (1971: 151) writes:

> The world of the mask is the world of the imaginary. The most astonishing formal inventions go along with an equally remarkable spontaneity in the ordering of the subject matter. It is likely that neither the spontaneity nor the formality is felt as such by either dancers and spectators. Even if a ceremony that includes masks interrupted by interludes or satiric or comic elements, it remains a sacred spectacle carrying out events that are considered real by the persons involved. To these ends, richly varied methods are employed. Realistic observation mingles with the fantastic; idealized facial forms coincide with often rigorously expressive ones.

In Assam's Vaishnavism, God is propitiated through different kinds of prayers and performances. The God appeased in this cult is described in different Vaishnavite scriptures. Lord Vishnu is the supreme god of the Vaishnavas, whose powers and virtues are focused and established through the act of different gods and goddesses. The mythological stories of the gods are depicted through various *bhaona* performed in the *satras* where different masks have been used. These masks are generally worn by different actors who perform the role of demons, incarnations of gods, animals, and so on. Often, masks are worn by some human characters to express perfectly vigour, tudicrousness, or dishonesty.

'Heritage of Mask at Majuli' is the fourth chapter of this thesis in which an attempt has been made to explore the art and skill of mask making, including its history and growth at the Natun Chamaguri Satra. In Assam, traditionally, masks have been made from different materials like bamboo, clay, sheath of areca nut plant, wood, etc., which are easily available in the surroundings of the mask makers. Till date, many artistic wooden masks are found in *satras* and other community centres of Assam. However, bamboo is the principal constituent material of the masks in the *satras* of Majuli. In the *satras,* mask makers usually make masks from bamboo splits, which are woven into a basket in open hexagonal pattern, covered with pieces of cotton fabrics, and a paste of *kumarmati,* a special kind of clay, mixed with cow-dung of the calf that is not weaned, and water. According to the mask makers, dung of such calves possess more adhesiveness than that of the other cows. Cow-dung is treated as a sacred element by the Hindus, and is used to purify a place or a person. However, in mask making it is used not for its sanctity, but for its adhesive quality. The mask makers who make mask by bamboo split are in better position than those who make mask from stone, wood, etc. The size of a stone or log restricts the imagination of the mask maker, and they are restricted to making masks according to the size of the material. In a mask made of split bamboo, they can add one after another bamboo split to materialize their imagination. Moreover, masks made of bamboo splits are lighter in comparison to those made of stone or wood. In olden days, the mask makers made their colours, brushes, etc. from natural objects. But because of the problems involved in the preparing process, and also because of non-availability of the natural materials in the surroundings, nowadays they have begun to use colours and brushes that are available in the market. However, till date broad brushes used for colouring masks are still made from the jute fiber fixed to bamboo sticks by the mask makers of the Natun Chamaguri Satra.

Tradition has immense control in the mask making process of the Natun Chamaguri Satra. It is evident, for example, in the making of the mask of Ravana. It is difficult to arrange ten heads of the demon king Ravana, because the actor who has to wear the mask has to insert his head into one of the heads of the mask. The other of the nine heads have to be arranged by the mask maker on both the sides of the head of the actor. It is a difficult task because if the maker arranged the mask in a row, five heads will be on one side and four will be on the other. If the mask is made in this manner, it will not be symmetrical and will lack aesthetic beauty. To get rid of such difficulties, mask makers of the Natun Chamaguri Satra make a big face of Ravana and arrange the other nine heads of smaller size more or less in a semi-circular manner above the principal head.

Sarkar (2001: 223) divides masks of North Bengal into the following categories:

1. Masks of mythological characters
2. Masks of Hindu gods and goddesses
3. Masks of malevolent spirits
4. Masks of common man and woman
5. Masks of animals and birds.

The masks of the Natun Chamaguri Satra can be divided into those of mythological characters, those of common men and women, and those of animals, birds, serpents, etc. The mask of Hindu gods and goddesses could be easily included in the category of the mythological characters. Both anthropomorphic and theriomorphic masks are found in the study *satra*. Moreover, there is mask like Narasimha, which is the combination of an anthropomorphic and theriomorphic forms.

The mask makers of the study *satra* make three types of masks: *mukh mukha, cho mukha,* and *lotokai* or *lotokari mukha.* The *mukh mukha* covers only the facial part of the wearer; the *cho mukha* is the biggest type of mask, and a combination of many separately made parts, which are tied from inside to the body of the wearer. The *lotokai mukha* is more or less same as *cho mukha* except it being comparatively smaller in size. All these masks are used in Vaishnavite theatrical performance according to the nature of the characters. Malik (2001: 52) writes:

> In the world of performance—dance, drama, music—for instance there are the theatrical masks, and those others meant for aesthetic and artistic purposes which allow for a multiple of expressions that may correspond with the mythological dimension. Often theatre masks reveal to the spectators insights and truth about ethic and the human condition. There are various methods in different cultures bringing out the three-dimensionality of forms of masks within the context of performances. In this way there is the unfolding of the inner personality at the deepest level, through active participation with the spectator who activates his/her own dormant imagination.

The above lines, in short, tell us about the traditional societies masks in dance, music, theatre, plays, drama, etc. reveal the mythological-collective unconscious dimensions which are reflected during various enactments of archetypes of images, e.g., heroes, demons, animals, sprits, ancestors, etc. In this case, masks are therefore indicators of the ideal ethical and aesthetic models and dreams in any particular society'.

Caste in Assam is basically not a functional division; relation of a caste with the traditional occupation is a flaccid factor in this state. There is no mask making caste in Assam. However, in the Natun Chamaguri Satra, all the mask makers are from the Kayastha caste, traditionally who were scribes of zamindars.

It is a known fact that masks made at *satras* of Majuli are principally used in *bhaonas.* Traditionally, different roles in a *bhaona* including those of females were performed by the males only. Nowadays, the female roles in such performances are sometimes done by the females. However, till date the roles of ferocious demonesses like Putana, Taraka, et al., which have to be performed invariably by wearing masks and integral elaborate costumes, are performed by the males only. After wearing a mask, a common man with whom the villagers have the face to face relation, becomes the mythological character; a good character becomes the centre of respect, while the bad characters evoke awe in the heart and mind of the spectators. 'In fact, throughout man's history, the religious function has been one of the most important in artistic production' (Conrad, 1967: 250). The masks in Assam are treated as living beings. It is also believed that the masks of ferocious demons and evil characters quarrel in darkness. To avoid such situations, earthen lamps are lit and incense sticks and incense powder are burnt at dusk in front of such masks. Some scholars opine that some of the masks evoke awe and reverence in the minds of spectators due to their huge size and grotesqueness. There are a good number of masks of huge size at the Natun Chamaguri Satra, particularly most of the *cho mukhas,* all of which are not greatly honoured by the people; on the other hands the masks of Kalinaga, Narasimha, Ravana, etc. are greatly revered. Narasimha is the incarnation of Lord Vishnu, and for its mythological affiliation it is adored and revered by the community. Surprisingly enough, evil characters like the serpent king Kalinaga and the demon king Ravana are also greatly revered. Probably, it is due to the fact that both these characters, although basically malevolent, were controlled and killed by two incarnations of Lord Vishnu, i.e., Krishna and Rama, respectively. In a fight Krishna defeated Kalinaga and the malacious serpent had to leave the lake he used as his abode and made water poisonous adding his deadly venom. Before leaving the lake, he submitted himself completely to Lord Vishnu, and promised not to cause any harm to any being. Basically, Ravana was a pious demon; he was also wise and a good sitarist. His arrogance and pride led him to abduct Sita, and for that misdeed he was killed by Rama, and his golden kingdom was ruined. Before his death, he admitted the power and superiority of Rama, and received benediction from this incarnation of Lord Vishnu. Perhaps due to the concept of 'good triumphs over evil', and 'evil submits before good', the masks of Kalinaga and Ravana are revered by the people.

Masks are always associated with taboos and rituals. Before wearing a mask in a ritualistic performance, particularly before wearing the revered masks, the performers have to go through fasting and such other taboos. It is believed that breach of taboos invariably brings distress to the performers and also to the villagers. According to the inhabitants of the Natun Chamaguri, many incidents occured in the performance of the *bhaonas* for not observing the prescribed taboos by the actors. It is also believed that masks should be made according to the description of the scriptures following the tradition prevailing in the *satra*. People believe that disobeying of such strictures bring misfortune during the performance of a *bhaona*. Ritual is an important component of a *bhaona*; however, masks, dances, songs, etc. are not subordinate to ritualism.

Chapter V of the thesis is devoted to the description of the available masks of the Natun Chamaguri Satra. A good number of masks found in the *satra* are splendid and wonderful creations of craftsmanship and are objects of great aesthetic beauty. It is pertinent to note here that all the masks made in the *satra* are the exact representations of the scripture's descriptions, for which one can observe the structural differences of Narasimha of Majuli with that of other parts of India. All these masks are made by five mask makers only, all of whom are male and consanguinally related to the *satradhikar's* lineage.

Although females are not tabooed to make masks, not a single woman of the study village has adopted this skill. In many societies, masks are used to drive away the evil spirits, cure diseases and ailments, etc.; however, the masks found in the Natun Chamaguri Satra are without any touch of such magical fervour. It is a universal concept that mask is a being that protects the wearer. Furthermore, in many societies, masks are used to protect people from wrongdoers, black magicians, and witches. For the members of secret, societies masks become the implement of political pressure. The actors of *bhaona* at the study *satra* strongly believe that if they wear masks strictly observing the prescribed taboos, the masks protect them at least during the performance of a ritual play. It is also believed by the people that a revered mask like Narasimha, Ravana, etc. protects the *satra* from all evils. The people of the tribal and backward societies had deep metaphoric function in their pristine masks. They became supernatural and acquired the nature and power of the animals, demons and deities, by putting on such masks. In the study *satra* also, people believe that by wearing a mask of a mighty mythological god, demon, incarnation, etc., one automatically acquires power and vigour of that character.

'Just as the mediums used in art vary from society to society, so do the temperaments, needs, and personalities of the artists. No two men have identical emotions, perceptions, and skills. Whatever the art form or the material employed, variations in the finished product will come from the artist himself' (Conrad, 1964: 236). The mask of the Natun Chamaguri Satra is basically made from bamboo splits; the forms and features of these masks are derived from the scriptures obeying the norms and values of the society. Yet, different masks of a mythological character made by different mask makers vary according to the imagination and aesthetic sensibility of the makers; the expert maker with his adept fingers makes splendid masks, while in the hands of some other makers masks do not get the desired shape. Probably, the best known of all magically related art form is the mask. In a mask, factors like aesthetics, status, religion, etc. are conglomerated. When a common man wears the mask of the ten-headed, twenty-handed, mighty demon-king Ravana, he loses his self and becomes the epitome of awe and vigour. His status is immediately changed from a common man to a powerful king. Losing one's status and acquiring another identity by wearing a particular mask is a common belief in a religious atmosphere. If the same person wears the mask of a tiger or a common demon, his acquired status will be different. The mask makers are respected in society, but they are not paid well for their skill. In the Natun Chamaguri village, most of the mask makers make masks to fulfil their aesthetic urge, and to maintain their families they have to depend on other economic pursuits.

The use of mask is a very fundamental element in the traditional dance and dramas of innumerable societies of the world. In such societies, the use of masks is not only theatrical, but also possesses deep roots in the religious matrix. 'Masks are powerful because they do not disclose any emotion and change. In a certain sense, masks intimate immorality' (Kak, 2001: 18). The masks of Majuli have a thought-provoking tradition. Many mask makers of this riverine island, particularly the mask makers of the Natun Chamaguri Satra, are the bearers of this splendid art form; many of them have also added new aesthetic dimensions to this age-old skill, and for that, although not economically, they are praised by the people in and outside of the state. This art form has attracted many people in and outside the island, but unfortunately only a few number of persons have acquired this skill as principal economic pursuit because of the meagre income from mask making. 'Mask form a very significant mode of creative expression of all cultures. This is one of the many ways in which culture have given expression to their artistic faculties. These range from the use of mask in theatre and performance, to the use of the metaphor in visual expression as literary discourse' (Malik, 2001: XXX-XXXI). In Vaishnavism of Assam, without mask some of the prescribed propitiations could not be conducted. The Vaishnava cult of Assam is very rich in literature, and there are some scriptures which are adorned with colourful paintings. However, in those books not a single figure is seen wearing a mask. We cannot ignore the indispensable relation of masks with Assam's Vaishnavism. Although there are many negative factors associated with the skill of mask making, yet due to its integral relation with Vaishnavism, it will be practised by the people of Assam, at least in the precincts of the *satras.*

Bibliography

A Committee of the Royal Anthropological Institute of Great Britain and Ireland, 1954, Notes and Queries on Anthropology (6th edition), Routledge and Kegan Paul Ltd., London.

Abbate, Francesco (ed.), 1972, *African Art and Oceanic Art*, Octopus Books, London.

Adam, L., 1942, *Primitive Art*, Penguin Books, New York.

Adams, Edward B., 1979, *Art Treasure of Seoul*, Seoul International Tourist Publishing, Korea.

Ahuja, Ram, 2008 (Reprint), *Research Methods*, Rawat Publication, New Delhi.

Amatya, Saphalya, 1991, *Art and Culture of Nepal: An Attempt towards Preservation*, Nirala Publications, Jaipur.

Ambesi, Alberto Cerase, 1970, *Oceanic Art*, Hamlyn House, The Hamlyn Publishing Group Ltd., London.

Ambrose, Kay, 1983, *Classical Dances and Costumes of India*, Revised by Ram Gopal, Adam and Charles Black, London: xii.

Anand, Mulk Raj, 1968, Chhau Dance—Andaman, in *Marg* 22(I): 2-4.

Anati, Emmanuel and Ariela Fradkin Anati, 2001, Mind, Man and Mask in Prehistoric Art, in S.C. Malik (ed.) *Rupa - Pratirupa: Mind Man and Mask*, Indira Gandhi National Centre for the Arts, New Delhi: 107-109.

Anderson, Janathan, Berry H. Durston and Millicent Poole, 1992, *Thesis and Assignment Writing*, Willy Eastern Ltd., New Delhi.

Aryan, K.C., 1991, *Indian Folk Bronzes*, Rekha Prakashan, New Delhi.

Aryan, Subhashini, 1993, *Crafts of Himachal Pradesh*, Mapin Publishing, Ahmedabad.

Aubert, Laurent, 1980, The Swiss Folkloric Masks, in *The World of Music, 22 (I)*, Special Issue on Mask: 53-68.

Baker, Susan (ed.), 1992, *Myths and Legends*, New Burlington Books, London.

Bancroft-Hunt, Norman, 1988, *People of the Totem: The Indians of the Pacific Northwest*, Little Brown and Co., London.

Banerji, Projesh, 1982, *Aesthetics of Indian Folk-Dance*, Cosmos Publications, New Delhi.

Barbier, Jean Paul, 2000, Artifact and Artifice: Remarks by a Lucid, if Not Infallible, in *Arts and Cultures, No.1*: 150-170.

Barkataki, S., 1969, *Assam*, National Book Trust, New Delhi.

——, 1981, *Assam at a Glance*, Bani Prakash, Gauhati.

Barua, Birinchi Kumar, 1950, *A Cultural History of Assam*, Guwahati.

——, 1994, *Sankardeva: The Vaishnava Saint of Assam*, Guwahati.

Barua, Hem., 1965, *Assamese Literature*, National Book Trust, New Delhi.

Basu, M.N., 1961, *Field Method in Anthropology and Other Social Sciences*, Bookland Pvt. Ltd., Calcutta.

Beals, Ralph L., Harry Hoijer and Alen R. Beals, 1971, *An Introduction to Anthropology*, MacMillan Publishing Co. Inc., New York.

Behague, Gerard, 1980, South American Mask Dance: An Overview, in *The World of Music 22(1)*, Special Issue on Mask: 23-25.

Bell, J., 1999, *Doing Your Research Project*, Viva Books Private Ltd., New Delhi.

Ben-Amos, Paula Girshick, 1995, *The Art of Benin (2nd ed.)*, British Museum Publication, London.

Berger, Patricia and Terese Tse Bartholomew, 1995, *Mongolia: The Legacy of Chinggis Khan*, Thames and Hudson, XI, London.

Bhagabati, Abani Kumar, 2001, Biodiversity and Associated Problems in the Islands of the Brahmaputra, Assam, in *Geographical Review of India, Vol. 63, No. 4*: 330-43.

Bhagabati, Abani Kumar, Ashok K. Bora and Bimal K. Kar (eds.), 2001, *Geography of Assam*, Rajesh Publications, New Delhi.

Bhagabati, Annada C., 1994, Research Methods in Social Anthropology, *Bulletin of the Department of Anthropology, Gauhati University, Vol. VIII*: 1-5.

Bhagabati, S., 2001, *Assam at a Glance*, Bani Prakash, Gauhati.

Bhattacharyya, Asutosh, 1972, *Chhau Dance of Purulia*, Rabindra Bharati University, Calcutta, VIII.

Bhavnani, Enakshi, 1974, *Folk and Tribal Designs of India*, Taraporevala, Bombay.

Biebuyck, Daniel P., 1969, *Tradition and Creativity in Tribal Art*, University of California Press, Berkeley and Los Angeles.

Biswas, D.P. and G.C. Ojah, 2002, Pure Occupation with Impure Social Status: A Study of the Hiras (A Scheduled Caste in Assam), *The Journal of Anthropological Survey of India, Vol. 51, No. 3*: 105-124.

Boas, Franz, 1955, *Primitive Art,* Dover Publication INC., New York.

Bohannan, Paul, 1964, *Africa and Africans,* Natural History Place, New York.

Bondi, Hermann, Alan Bullock, W. Gordon East, David Piper and Bernard Williams, 1969, *Art Across the World*, Marshall Convendish Books Ltd., London.

Bonnefoy, Yves (Compiled), 1981, *Mythologies, Vol. I,* Translated by Gerald Honigsblum, The University of Chicago Press, Chicago.

——, (Compiled), 1981, *Mythologies*, Vol. II, Translated by Gerald Honigsblum, The University of Chicago Press, Chicago.

Borkataki, S., 1969, *Assam,* National Book Trust, New Delhi.

Bouissac, Paul, 2001, Becoming a Mask: Facial Make-up and the Transformation of Identities, in S.C. Malik (ed.), *Rupa-Pratirupa: Mind, Man and Mask,* Indira Gandhi National Centre for the Arts, New Delhi: 73-80.

Bouquet, A.C., 1966, *Hinduism,* Hutchinson, London.

Bowie, Theodore (ed.), 1960, *The Arts of Thailand: A Handbook of the Architecture, Sculpture and Painting of Thailand (Siam) and a Catalogue of the Exhibition in the United States in 1960-61-62,* Indiana University, Bloomington.

Bowra, C.M., 1966, *Classical Greece,* Time Life International, Netherlands.

Brakel, Koos Van, David Van Duuren and Itie Van Hout, 1996, *A Passion for Indonesian Art,* Translated from the Dutch by Karen Gamester et al., Royal Tropical Institute, Amsterdam.

Brauen, Martin, 1980, *Feste in Ladakh,* Akademische Druck u Verlagsanstalt, Austria.

British Museum, 1922, *A Guide to the Babylonian and Assyrian Antiquities,* Harrison and Sons, London.

Burbank, Jon, 1991, *Nepal,* Times Books International, Singapore.

Campbell, Joseph, 1991, *The Masks of God: Primitive Mythology,* Penguin Books, Arkana.

Cantlie, Audrey, 1984, *The Assamese,* Curzon Press Ltd., London and Dublin.

Census of India, 1931, Vol. III, Assam.

Census of India, 1961, Vol. III, Assam: 211.

Census of India, 2001, *Provisional Population Totals: Assam*, Series 19, Paper 1 of 2001, Directorate of Census Operations, Assam.

Census of India, 2001, *Primary Census Abstract*, Directorate of Census Operations, Assam.

Chandavij, Natthapatra, and Prompom Pramualratana, 1998, *Thai Puppets and Khon Masks,* Thames and Hudson, London.

Chatterjee, Gautam, 1998, Living Heritage of Mask, in *Discover India-II*, 7: 14-19.

Chattopadhyay, Kamaladevi, 1976, *The Glory of Indian Handicrafts,* Indian Book Company, New Delhi.

——, 1985, *Handicrafts of India,* Indian Council of Cultural Relations, New Delhi.

Christensen, Erwin O., 1955, *Primitive Art*, Thomas Y. Crowell Co., New York.

Conrad, Jack, 1964, *The Many Worlds of Man*, MacMillan and Co. Ltd., London.

Coomaraswamy, Ananda K., 1965, *History of Indian and Indonesian Art*, Dover Publications, New York.
Cooper, Ilay and John Gillow, 1996, *Art and Crafts of India*, Thames and Hudson, London.
Cordwell, Justine M., 1959, African Art, in William R. Bascom and Melville J. Herskovits (ed.), *Continuity and Change*, Phoenix Books, The University of Chicago Press, Chicago: 28-48.
Dalton, A.C., 1851, Notes on the 'Mahapurusiyas': A Sect of Vaishnavism in Assam, *The Journal of the Asiatic Society of Bengal*, No. XX: 455-69.
Das, A.K., 2001, Myth and Manifestation, in S.C. Malik (ed.), *Rupa-Pratirupa: Mind, Man and Mask*, Indira Gandhi National Centre for the Arts, New Delhi: 176-82.
Das, B.M., 1967, A Note on the Races of Assam, in B.M. Das (ed.), *Kamrupa*, Souvenir, XII Session, All India Science Teachers' Association, Reception Committee, All India Science Teachers' Conference, Gauhati Session, Guwahati: 10-13.
Dasgupta, S.N., 1936, *History of Indian Philosophy*, Vol. II, Cambridge University.
——, 1949, *History of Indian Philosophy*, Vol. IV, Cambridge University.
Delange, Jacqueline, 1974, *The Art and Peoples of Black Africa*, Translated by Carol F. Jopling, E.P. Dutton and Co., XXVI, New York.
Deo, Juga Bhanu Singh, 1973, *Chhau: Mask Dance of Seraikela*, Cuttack.
Deva Goswami, P., 2001, The Satras of Majuli and Their Contribution, in *The Convention on Heritage Conservation: Majuli*: 17-18.
——, 2001, *Satria Utsavar Parichay aru Tatparya*, (Introduction and purposes of *satra* festivals), Kaustubh Prakashan, Dibrugarh.
Devi, Ragini, 1966, Festivals of the Goddess Bhagavati in Kerala, in *Marg* 19(2): 46-48.
Dey, Bishnu and John Irwin, 1947, The Folk Art of Bengal, in *Marg* 1(4): 45-54.
Dhamija, Ram, 1966, Masks, in *Marg* 20(I): 42.
Dhaninivat, Kromamun Bidyalabh Bridhyakorn and Dhanit Yupho, 1954, *The Khon*, The National Culture Institute: 16 (Thailand Culture Series; No. II), Bangkok.
Dowson, John, 1987, *A Classical Dictionary of Hindu Mythology and Religion, Geography, History, and Literature*, Rupa and Co., New Delhi.
Duerden, Dennis, 1970, *African Art*, The Hamlyn Publishing Group Ltd., London.
Dutta, Keshab Narayan, 1958, *Culture and Civilization of Assam*, Srimanta Sankara Kristi Bikash Samiti, Guwahati.
Dutta, Lila, 2003, *Amar Asam (Our Assam)*, Guwahati.
Elisseeff, Danielle and Vadime Elisseeff, 1985, *Art of Japan*, Translated from the French by I. Mark Paris, Harry N. Abrams. New York.
Elwin, V., 1951, *The Tribal Art of Middle India: A Personal Record*, Oxford University Press, London.

——, 1959, Regional Dances: Orissa. Dormitory Performance of the Murias, in *Marg* 13 (I): 64-68.
——, 1964, *A Philosophy for NEFA*, Advisor to the Government of Assam, Shillong.
——, 1969, *The Art of North-East India*, North-East Frontier Agency, Shillong.
Emigh, John, 1981, Masking and Playing: Observations on Masked Performance in New Guinea, in *The World of Music* 23 (3), Special Issue on Masks II: 5-21.
——, 1996, *Masked Performance: The Play of Self and Other in Ritual and Theatre*, University of Pennsylvania Press, Philadelphia: XVII.
Encyclopedia Americana: International Edition, 1981, Mask, Grolier Incorporated, USA, V.18: 423-26.
Endo, Toru, 1994, The Bugaku Tradition in Japanese Folk Performing Arts, in *Journal of Association for Indian Music Society*, No. 4: 76-91.
Eyo, Ekpo, 1990, *Two Thousand Years of Nigerian Art*, Ethnographica, London.
Fagg, Bernard, 1990, *Nok Terracottas*, Ethnographica, London.
Feest, Christian F., 1994, *Native Arts of North America*, Thames and Hudson, London.
Fenton, William N., 1987, *The False Faces of The Iroquois*, University of Oklahoma Press, Norman, XXI.
Fienup-Riordan, Ann, 1996, *The Living Tradition of Yupik Masks: Agayuli-Yararput* (Our way of making prayer), Translated by Marie Meade, University of Washington Press, London.
Fischer, Eberhard and Hans Himmelheber, 1984, *The Arts of the Dan in West Africa*, Museum Rietberg, Zurich, Switzerland.
Fischer, Joseph, 1994, *The Folk Art of Java*, Oxford University Press, Oxford, XV.
Furer-Haimendorf, Christopher Von, 1972, *The Sherpas of Nepal: Buddhist Highlanders*, Vikas Publishing House, New Delhi.
Gait, Sir Edward, 2005 (Reprint), *A History of Assam*, LBS Publication, Guwahati.
Galerie, Simone De Monbrison, 1952, *Arts Antiques—Arts Primitifs*, Paris.
Gargi, Balwant, 1991, *Folk Theatre of India*, Rupa and Co., Allahabad, X.
Ghosh, B.N., 2006 (Reprint), *Scientific Method and Social Research*, Sterling Publishers Pvt. Ltd., New Delhi.
Ghurye, G.S., 1965, *Religious Conciousness*, Popular Prakashan, Bombay.
Gillison, Gillian, 1977, Fertility Rites and Sorcery in a New Guinea Village, in *National Geographic* 152(1): 124-46.
——, 1983, Living Theatre in New Guinea's Highlands, in *National Geographic* 164 (No.2): 147-69.
Gillon, Werner, 1979, *Collecting African Art*, London.
Gohain, Hiren, 2005, *Majulir Jilingani* (The Gleams of Majuli), Banalata, Guwahati.
Golub, Mort, 1999, Transforming Masks: Masks of Himalayas, in *Arts of Asia*, 29(2): 65-77.

Goode, W.J. and P.K. Hatt, 1981, *Methods in Social Research*, McGraw-Hill International Book Co., New Delhi.

Goswami, Krishna, 2001, Majulir Mukha Silpar Parampara Aru Carcha (Tradition and Practice of Mask at Majuli), in *Majuli,* Prasanta Kr. Sarma (ed.), New Era Media Service, Jorhat: 141-43.

Goswami, N., 2001, Majulir satrasamuhar aitihya aru samskritik parikrama, (Heritage and Cultural Acceleration of the *Satras* of Majuli), in *The Souvenir (Convention on Heritage Conservation: Majuli).*

Gouissac, Paul, 2001, Becoming a Mask: Facial Make-up and the Transformation of Identities, in *Rupa-Pratirupa: Mind, Man and Mask,* S.C. Malik (ed.), Indira Gandhi National Centre for the Arts, New Delhi: 73-80.

Graham, Ian, 1986, Looters Rob Graves and History, in *National Geographic,* 169 (No. 4): 452-61.

Grolier International Encyclopedia, 1991, African Art, Grolier Incorporated, Vol. I, Danburry: 160c-160g.

——, 1991, Masks, Grolier Incorporated, Danbury, Vol. 13: 196-98.

Grund, Francoise, 1985, *Chhau Dance*, House of World Cultures, France: 133 (Art of India).

Grund, Francoise, 1985, *Dances Chhau*, Maison Des Cultures Du Monde, France: 133 (Arts De L'Inde).

Hamilton, Francis, 1940, *An Account of Assam*, ed. by S.K. Bhuyan, Department of Historical and Antiquarian Studies, Gauhati, Assam.

Helffer, Mireille, 1980, The Cham of Padmasambhava in the Monastery of Hemis (Ladakh), in *The World of Music,* 22 (I), Special issue on Mask: 107-21.

Heppell, Michael, 1992, *Masks of Kalimantan*, Indonesian Arts Society, Melbourne.

Hersey, Irwin, 1991, *Indonesian Primitive Art*, Oxford University Press, Singapore: xvii.

Horcasitas, Fernando, 1978, Mexican Folk Art, in *National Geographic*, 153 (No. 5): 648-69.

Indira Gandhi National Centre for the Arts, 2002, *Vinhangama*, Newsletter, New Delhi, Vol. 5.

Ions, Veronica, 1987, *The World's Mythology*, Hamlyn, England.

Iteanu, Andre, 1981, Masked Plays in Oceania, in *The World of Music,* 23 (3), Special issue on Masks II: 26-33.

Jay, Sian E., 2001, The Mark Gordon Collection of South East Asian Tribal Sculpture, *Arts of Asia,* 30(1): 54-70.

Judge, Joseph, 1978, Minoans and Mycenaeans: Greece's Brilliant Bronze Age, in *National Geographic,* 153 (No.2): 142-85.

Jungwiwattanaporn, Parichat, 1999, Contemporary Theatre in Thailand: A Profile, in *SPAFA Journal, 9* (No.2): 5-14.

Kak, Subhash, 2001, Mind, Immortality and Art, in S.C. Malik (ed.), *Rupa-Pratirupa: Mind, Man and Mask,* Indira Gandhi National Centre for the Arts, New Delhi: 16-27.

Kakati, Banikanta, 1967 (Reprint), *Mother Goddess Kamakhya*, Lawyer's Book Stall, Guwahati.

——, 1956, *Purani Kamrupar Dharmar Dhara* (The Trend of Religion in Ancient Kamrupa), Bani Prakash Mandir, Guwahati.

Kartiwa, Suwati, 1990, *Topeng Traditional Indonesia Dan Asean: Indonesian and Asean Traditional Masks*, Museum Nasional, Jakarta.

Keay, John, 1986, *Ladakh: Land of the Passes*, Wienand Verlag, Germany.

Keng Yan Jun (ed.), 1990, *No Mask: A Book of Mask Opera*, Xu Sheng Chu Ben Shi, Taiwan.

Kerchache, Jacques, Jean Lovis Paudral and Lucien Stephan, 1993, *Art of Africa*, Harry N. Abrams, New York.

Khokar, Mohan, 1959, Regional Dances: Kerala, in *Marg* 13 (I): 38-41.

——, 1981, Chaitra Parva Rituals: Chhau Dances, in *Marg* 34(3): 74-87.

——, 1986, *Tradition of Indian Classical Dance*, 3rd edn., Clarion Books, New Delhi.

——, 1989, Thiyan, in *Sangeet Natak*, No. 94: 26-32.

Konishi, Masatoshi A., 1997, Masks and Performing Arts: India and Japan, in *Journal of Association for Indian Music Society*, No. 6: 43-55.

Kothari, C.R., 2004, *Research Methodology: Methods and Techniques* (2nd edn.), New Age International Publishers, New Delhi.

Kothari, Sunil, 1968, Chhau Dances of Saraikella, in *Marg* 22(I): 5-24.

——, 1979, Kathakali: The Sacred Dance Drama of Kerala, in *Splendours of Kerala*, Marg Publications, Bombay: 81-91.

——, 1980, The Use of Masks in Indian Dances and Dance Dramas, *The World of Music* 22(I), Special issue on Masks: 89-103.

Kurath, Gertrude Prokosch, 1981, Masked Dances of Native North America, in *The World of Music* 23(3), Special issue on Mask II: 58-66.

Landau, Sidney I (Editor in Chief), 2000, *The New International Webster's Student Dictionary of the English Language*, CBS Publishers and Distributors, New Delhi.

Laude, Jean, 1971, *The Art of Black Africa*, University of California Press, London.

Lechuga, Ruth D. and Sayer Chloe, 1994, *Mask Art of Mexico*, Chronicle Books, San Francisco.

Leiris, Michael and Jacqueline Delange, 1968, *African Art*, Translated by Michael Ross, Thames and Hudson, London, XI: 454 (The Art of Mankind, ed. by Andre Malraux and Andre Parrot.)

Leuzinger, Elsy, 1960, *Africa: The Art of the Negro Peoples*, Translated by Ann E. Keep, Methuen, London.

Leuzinger, Elsy, 1967, *The Art of Africa: The Art of the Negro People*, Grestone Press, New York: 239.

Levi-Strauss, Claude, 1977, *Structural Anthropology* (Translated from French by Claire Jacobson and Brooke Grundfest Schoepf), The Penguin Press, Great Britain.

——, 1983, *The Way of the Mask* (La Voie des Masques), Translated by Sylvia Modelski, University of Washington Press, London.

Locke, Elizabeth and Sheila Savill, 1976, Classical Greece and Rome, Narrative Outlines: Greece Legends of the House of Peoples, in *Pears Encyclopedia of Myths and Legends*, Mary Barker and Christopher Cook (ed.), VI, Pelham Books, London: 180-86.

Macdonald, Nicole Revel, 1981, Masks in Kalimantan Timur, in *The World of Music*, 23 (3), Special issue on Mask, II: 52-56.

Mack, John (ed.), 1994, *Masks: The Art of Expression*, British Museum, London.

Mahanta, Pradip Jyoti, 2001, Viewing the World through the Masks of Assam, in S.C. Malik (ed.), *Rupa-Pratirupa: Mind Man and Mask*, Indira Gandhi National Centre for the Arts, New Delhi: 171-75.

Mahanta, Prasanta Kumar (ed.), 2001, *Majuli*, Grantha Samaskriti, Jorhat.

Malik, S.C. (ed.), 2001, *Rupa-Pratirupa: Mind Man and Mask*, Indira Gandhi National Centre for the Arts, New Delhi.

Malik, S.C., 2001, Mask: A Question of Self-identity—What Tradition Reveals Modernity Conceals, in S.C. Malik (ed.), *Rupa-Pratirupa: Mind Man and Mask*, Indira Gandhi National Centre for the Arts, New Delhi: 50-72.

Maquet, Jacques, 1972, *Africanity: The Cultural Unity of a Black Africa*, Oxford University Press, New York.

Mark, Peter, 1992, *The Wild Bull and The Sacred Forest: Form, Meaning and Change in Senegambian Initiation Masks*, Cambridge University Press, Cambridge, XIII.

Martin, K.K., 1970, Indigenous Theatre in West Africa, in *Sangeet Natak*, No.18 (Oct-Dec.): 52-72.

Massey, Reginald and Jamila Massey, 1989, *The Dances of India: A General Survey and Dancers' Guide*, Tricolour Books, London, XIX: 164.

McDowell, Bart, 1980, The Aztecs, in *National Geographic*, 158 (No.6): 704-752.

McCune, Evelyn, 1962, *The Arts of Korea: An Illustrated History*, Charles E. Tuttle Company, Japan: 452.

Medhi, Birinchi K., 2003, a. Ajan udar satradhikarar sannidhyat, in *Dainik Asam*, Guwahati: Chandmari, 23rd June: 4.

——, 2003, b. Matrika Majuli, in *Asam Bani*, Guwahati, 27th June: 7.

——, 2003, c. Majulir Mukha, in *Amar Asam*, Guwahati, G.S. Road, Ulubari, 2 July: 4.

——, 2003, d. Paranggat mukha khanikar Hem Chandra Goswami, in *Prantik*, Guwahati, Chandmari, 16-31 July, 1600 issue: 3.

——, 2003, e. Majulir Maydanava, in *Saptahik Janambhumi*, Guwahati, 6 August: 2.

——, 2003, f. Pratibandheer parakashtha, in *Dainik Asam*, Guwahati, 13 August: 6.

——, 2003, g. Behind the Mask, in *The Assam Tribune*, Guwahati, Tribune Buildings, Chandmari, 29th August.

——, 2004, Mukha sambandhe jatkinchit, in *Nree Barta*, Anthropological Society of Dudhnoi College, Dudhnoi, Vol.I, No.3: 5-6.

——, 2006, Mukha (mask) in Md. Taher (ed.), *Viswakosh: Samaj aru Samskriti* (Encyclopedia: Society and Culture), Assam Sahitya Sabha, Jorhat: 585-586.

——, 2008, Concept of Jagannatha among the Assamese Hindus, in R.N.Dash (ed.) *Jagannatha in Historical Perspective,* Pratibha Prakashan, Delhi: 90-102.

Medhi, Birinchi K. and Arifur Zaman, 2004, Mask Makers of a Vaishnavite Monastery of Assam, *The Journal of North-East India Council for Social Science Research,* Vol. 28, No.I: 4-8.

——, 2008, Tradition of Mask at a Vaishnavite Monastery in Majuli of Assam, in Kishore K. Basa and Birinchi K. Medhi (ed.), *Intangible Cultural Heritage of Assam,* Intangible Heritage of India, Series-6, Indira Gandhi Rashtriya Manav Sangrahalaya, Bhopal: 213-24.

Merton D. Simpson, 1966, *African Excellence,* New York: 24.

Miettinen, Jukka O. 1992, *Classical Dance and Theatre in South-East Asia,* Oxford University Press, XX.

Miller, Mary Ellen, 1993, *The Art of Mesoamerica: From Olmec to Aztec*, Thames and Hudson, London.

Mode, Heiz, and Subodh Chandra, 1985, *Indian Folk Art,* Alpine Fine Arts Collection, New York.

Modelski, Sylvia, 1982, *The Way of the Masks* (English Translation of the Claude Levi-Strauss' book *La Voie des Masques*), University of Washington Press, Seattle.

Monte, F., 1969, *African Masks,* The Hamlyn Publishing Group Ltd., Hamlyn House, London.

Mookerjee, Ajit, 1965, Survey of Some Important Museum of India: Crafts Museum, *Marg* 19(I): 18-20.

Moser, C.A.S and G. Kalton, 1971, *Survey Methods in Social Investigation,* English Language Book Society and Heinemann Educational Books Ltd., London.

Mullan: *Census of India, Vol III, Assam,* 1931: 113 (General).

Munsterberg, Hugo, 1968, *Art of the Far East,* Harry N. Abrams, New York.

Nair, D. Appukuttan, 1993, Rasabhinaya, in *Marg* 45 (I): 45-52.

Napier, A. David, 1986, *Masks, Transformation and Paradox,* University of California Press, Berkeley, XXVI: 282.

Neog, Maheswar, 1959, Regional Dances: Assam, *Marg* 13(I): 9-20.

——, 1965, *Sankaradeva and His Times,* Gauhati University Publication, Guwahati.

——, (ed.), 1969, *Pavitra Asam* (The Sacred Assam), Asam Sahitya Sabha, Jorhat.

——, 1984, *Religions of the North-East,* Munshiram Manohorlal Pvt. Ltd., New Delhi.

——, 1998, *The Contribution of Sankaradeva Movement to the Culture and Civilization of India*, Lawyer's Book Stall, Guwahati.

Nicholson, Irene, 1983, *Mexican and Central American Mythology*, The Standard Literature Co., India.

Nooter, Mary H., 1993, *Secrecy: African Art that Conceals and Reveals*, The Museum for African Art, New York.

Ojo, J.R.O., 1981, Masked Dances of the Yoruba Peoples, in *The World of Music*, 23 (3), Special issue on Mask II: 37-48.

Osborne, Harold, 1968, *South American Mythology*, Paul Hamlyn, Middlesex.

Paine, Robert Treat, and Alexander Soper, 1974, *The Art and Architecture of Japan*, 2nd edn., Penguin Books, England.

Pakyntein, E.H., 1961, *Census of India, 1961, Vol. III, Assam, Part I, A General Report.*

Pal, Pratapaditya, 1991, *Art of the Himalayas: Treasures from Nepal and Tibet*, Hudson Hills Press, New York.

Pande, B.M., 2001, Archaeology of Mask: Indian Evidence, in S.C. Malik (ed.), *Rupa-Pratirupa: Mind Man and Mask*, Indira Gandhi National Centre for the Arts, New Delhi: 50-72.

Pani, Jiwan, 1968, Chhau Dances of Mayurbhan, *Marg*, 22(I): 30-45.

——, 1969, Chhau: A Comperative Study of Sareikela and Mayurbhanj Forms, in *Sangeet Natak*, No. 13 (July-Sept.): 35-45.

——, 1986, *World of Other Faces: Indian Masks*, Publications Division, Ministry of Information and Broadcasting, Government of India, New Delhi.

Pannikar, Kavalam Narayana, 1979, Ecstasy of the Folk Dance—The Mystical Rhythms of the Village Community, in *Spendours of Kerala*, Marg Publications, Bombay: 107-10.

Parke-Bernet Galleries, 1966, *African and Oceanic Art*, New York.

Pate, Alan, 1998, Devil Dance Masks of Sri Lanka, in *Arts of Asia*, 28(5): 85-95.

Patnaik, D.N., 1997, The Chhau Dance of Mayurbhanj: I, *Sangeet Natak*, No. 125-126: 19-30.

——, 1998, The Chhau Dance of Mayurbhanj: II, *Sangeet Natak*, No. 127-28: 59-74.

——, 1999, The Chhau Dance of Mayurbhanj: III, *Sangeet Natak*, 131-132: 21-43.

Pelto, Pertti J. and Gretel H. Pelto, 1978, *Anthropological Research: The Structure of Inquiry* (2nd edn.), Cambridge University Press, London.

Piggot, Juliet, 1982, *Japanese Mythology*, The Standard Literature Co., India.

Pinitpouvadd, Sidtha, 1999, The Ghost Festival of Phee Ta Khon, in *SPAFA Journal 9*: 23-28.

Plekhnanov, G.V., 1953, *Art and Social Life*, People's Publishing House Ltd., Bombay.

Population Research Centre, 1995, *National Family Health Survey: 1992-1993*, Population Research Centre, Guwahati.

Puri, B.N., 1968, *Studies in Early History and Administration in Assam*, Department of Publications, Gauhati University, Guwahati.

Putman, John J., 1985, Those Eternal Austrians, in *National Geographic*, 167 (No. 4): 410-49.

Radhakrishnan, S., 1959, *Religion and Society*, Jorge Allen and Unwin Ltd., London.

Rajakaruna, D.A., 1993, The Classical Noh Theatre of Japan: An Indian Approach, in *Sangeet Natak* 108-09: 17-22.

Richards, David, 1994, *Masks of Difference: Cultural Representation in Literature, Anthropology and Art*, Cambridge University Press, Cambridge, XII: 348.

Rowland, Benjamin, 1970, *The Pelican History of Art*, Penguin Books Inc., Baltimore.

Roy, Sankar Kumar, 1985, A Report on the Mask Preserved in the Anthropological Museum, Department of Anthropology, Gauhati University, in *The Assam Academic Review*, Special Vol., No. 2, 1984-85: 57-65.

Saikia, Nagen (ed.), 1980, *Assam and the Assamese Mind*, Asam Sahitaya Sabha, Chandrakanta Handique Bhavan, Jorhat, Assam.

Sannes, G.W., 1970, *African 'Primitives': Function and Form in African Masks and Figures*, Translated by Margaret King, Faber and Faber, London.

Saraf, D.N., 1985, *Indian Crafts: Development and Potential*, 2nd revised edn., Vikas Publishing House, Ghaziabad.

Sarkar, Sabita Ranjan, 2001, Mask of West Bengal: An Anthropological Study, in S.C. Malik (ed.), *Rupa-Pratirupa: Mind, Man and Mask*, Indira Gandhi National Centre for the Arts, New Delhi: 221-31.

Sarma, S.N., 1999, *The Neo-Vaishnavite Movement and the Satra Institution of Assam*, Lawyer's Book Stall, Guwahati.

Savill, Sheila, 1977, Ancient Iran and the Indian Sub-continent: Endex and Glossary, in Mary Barker and Christopher Cook (ed.), *Pears Encyclopedia of Myths and Legends*, Pelham Books, London, V.3: 97-130.

——, 1978, The Americans: Index and Glossary, in Mary Barker and Christopher Cook (ed.), *Pears Encyclopedia of Myths and Legends*, Pelham Books, London, V.4: 189-222.

Sen, Prabhas, 1994, *Crafts of West Bengal*, Mapin Publishing, Ahmedabad.

Sharer, Robert J., 1994, *The Ancient Maya* (5th ed.), Standard University Press, California.

Singh, Jaspal, 1991, *Introduction to Methods of Social Research*, Sterling Publishers Pvt. Ltd., New Delhi.

Singh, Madanjit, 1970, *Himalayan Art*, The Macmillan Company of India Ltd., Bombay.

——, 1971, *Himalayan Art: Wall-Painting and Sculpture in Ladakh, Lahual and Spiti, the Siwalik Ranges, Nepal, Sikkim and Bhutan*, Macmillan, London: 287.

Sinha, Surajit, 1974, Sociology of Religion, in *A Survey of Research in Sociology and Social Anthropology*, Vol. II, ICSSR, New Delhi: 508-30.

Srinivas, M.N., 1952, *Religion and Society among the Coorgs of South India*, Asian Publishing House, New Delhi.

——, 1992, *Caste in Modern India and Other Essays*, Media Promoters & Publishers Pvt. Ltd., Bombay.

Stack, E., 1981, *Report on the Census of Assam*, India, Vol. III: 63.

The Mask Tradition of India, 2000, Marg Publication, Mumbai.

The New Encyclopaedia Britannica, 1991, Mask, Philip W. Goetz, Editor in Chief, Encyclopaedia Britanica, Inc., Chicago, Vol. 7: 910-11.

Trowell, Margaret, 1953, *Classical African Sculpture*, 2nd edn., Faber and Faber, London.

Underwood, Leon, 1948, *Masks of West Africa*, Alee Tiranti, London, VI.

Uppal, Hari, 1959, Regional Dances: Bihar, in *Marg* 13 (I): 26-30.

Vaillant, George C., 1966, *Aztecs of Mexico: Origin, Rise and Fall of The Aztec Nation*, Revised by Suzannah B. Vaillant, 2nd edn., Doubleday and Co., USA.

Vatsyayan, Kapila, 1980, *Traditional Indian Theatre: Multiple Streams*, National Book Trust, New Delhi, XI.

——, 1987, *Traditions of Indian Folk Dance*, 2nd revised and enlarged edn., Clarion Books, New Delhi, VI.

Venu, G., 1993, The Mask Dances of Kerala, in *Sangeet Natak* 108-109 (April-Sept.): 10-16.

Vergati, Anne, 1999, *Gods and Masks of the Kathmandu Valley*, D.K. Printworld, New Delhi, XII.

Vidyarthi, L.P., 1961, *The Sacred Complex of Hindu Gaya*, Asia Publishing House, Calcutta.

——, (ed.), 1962, *Aspects of Religion in Indian Society*, Kedarnath Ramnath, Meerut.

——, 1993, *Art and Culture of North-East India*, Publication Division, Ministry of Information and Broadcasting, Government of India, New Delhi.

Warren, William, and Luca Invernizzi Tettoni, 1994, *Arts and Crafts of Thailand*, Thames and Hudson, London, 45 (I): 4-26.

Warrier, Kalamandalam Govinda, 1993, Aharyabhinaya, in *Marg*, 45(I): 4-26.

Wassing, Rene S., 1970, *The Art of Africa*, Thames and Hudson, London.

Weruer, O. and G.M. Schoepfle, 1987, *Systematic Fieldwork*, Sage Publications, New Delhi.

Wilkinson, T.S. and P.L. Bhandarkar, 1977, *Methodology and Techniques of Social Research*, Himalaya Publishing House, Mumbai.

Williams, Denis, 1974, *Icon and Image: A Study of Sacred and Secular Forms of African Classical Art*, Allen Lane, London, XV.

Woldering, Irmgard, 1967, *Gods, Men and Pharaohs: The Glory of Egyptian Art*, Harry N. Abrams, New York, VII.

Wyatt, Gary, 1994, *Spirit Faces: Contemporary Masks of the North West Coast*, Douglas and McIntyre, Vancouver.

Young, Pauline V., 2001, *Scientific Social Survey and Research* (4th edn.), Prentice-Hall of India Pvt. Ltd., New Delhi.

Index